ROUTLEDGE LIBRARY EDITIONS:
MONETARY ECONOMICS

Volume 6

TEMPORARY MONETARY EQUILIBRIUM THEORY

TEMPORARY MONETARY EQUILIBRIUM THEORY

A Differentiable Approach

KUAN-PIN LIN

Routledge
Taylor & Francis Group
LONDON AND NEW YORK

First published in 1984 by Garland Publishing, Inc.

This edition first published in 2017
by Routledge
2 Park Square, Milton Park, Abingdon, Oxon OX14 4RN

and by Routledge
711 Third Avenue, New York, NY 10017

Routledge is an imprint of the Taylor & Francis Group, an informa business

British Library Cataloguing in Publication Data
A catalogue record for this book is available from the British Library

ISBN: 978-1-138-73264-3 (Set)
ISBN: 978-1-315-16457-1 (Set) (ebk)
ISBN: 978-1-138-74554-4 (Volume 6) (hbk)
ISBN: 978-1-315-18058-8 (Volume 6) (ebk)

Publisher's Note
The publisher has gone to great lengths to ensure the quality of this reprint but points out that some imperfections in the original copies may be apparent.

Temporary Monetary Equilibrium Theory

A Differentiable Approach

Kuan-Pin Lin

Garland Publishing, Inc.
New York & London, 1984

Library of Congress Cataloging in Publication Data

Lin, Kuan-Pin, 1948–
Temporary monetary equilibrium theory.
(Outstanding dissertations in economics)
Abstract of thesis (Ph.D.)—State University of New York at Stony Brook, 1977.
Bibliography: p.
1. Money—Mathematical models. 2. Equilibrium (Economics) 3. Differential topology. I. Title. II. Series.
HG221.3.L523 1984 332.4'0724 79-53823
ISBN 0-8240-4172-0

All volumes in this series are printed on acid-free, 250-year-life paper.

Printed in the United States of America

TEMPORARY MONETARY EQUILIBRIUM THEORY: A DIFFERENTIABLE APPROACH

by

Kuan-Pin Lin

August, 1977

TABLE OF CONTENTS

Page

ABSTRACT.. iii

ACKNOWLEDGMENTS.. v

Chapter I: INTRODUCTION.. 1

Chapter II: THE MODEL - A SPOT MONEY ECONOMY. 9

a. Basic Definitions.. 10

b. Expectation Functions.. 12

c. von Neumann-Morgenstern Utility Functions..... 15

d. Expected Utility Functions.. 22

Chapter III: THE SPACE OF MONEY ECONOMIES..... 30

a. Mathematical Preliminaries.. 31

b. Topological Structure of the Space of Money Economies.. 34

c. Two Concepts of Equilibrium.. 35

Chapter IV: MAIN THEOREMS.. 41

a. Genericity of Regular Money Economies........ 42

b. Local Uniqueness and Stability of Temporary Monetary Equilibrium.. 56

c. Existence of Temporary Monetary Equilibrium.. 61

Chapter V: AN EXTENTION - TEMPORARY MONETARY EQUILIBRIUM THEORY WITH SPOT AND FUTURES TRANSACTIONS.. 73

a. The Model.. 75

b. Main Theorems.. 87

Chapter VI: CONCLUSION: SUGGESTIONS FOR FUTURE RESEARCH.. 92

REFERENCES.. 95

Abstract of the Dissertation

TEMPORARY MONETARY EQUILIBRIUM THEORY:
A DIFFERENTIABLE APPROACH

by

Kuanpin Lin

Doctor of Philosophy

in

Economics

State University of New York at Stony Brook

1977

This thesis deals with a temporary monetary equilibrium theory under uncertainty in a differentiable framework. Using the techniques of differential topology recently introduced into the economics literature, one investigates the structure of the set of temporary monetary equilibria. In particular, one proves the properties of local uniqueness and stability of temporary equilibria for "almost all" money economies as well as the existence theorem for every money economy. By allowing changes of tastes, beliefs and endowments for each agent, the concept of "almost all" economies is introduced using a notion of transversality in differential topology. The local uniqueness can be obtained without assuming concavity of the utility functions for any agent, and the stability follows from an application of the implicit function theorem. Among other conditions, the agents' expectations of the future environment which in turn depend on the current and past observations of the economy play an important role in determining the existence of a temporary monetary equilibrium. The tool of proving existence in this differentiable setting is degree theory in differential topology. This model can be extended in many directions. To explore money economies with future contracts, for example, one assumes that markets are known to reopen in the future and hence similar determinate equilibrium properties are established.

ACKNOWLEDGMENT

I wish to express my indebtedness to Professor Peter J. Kalman, my advisor, for his encouragement and supervision throughout this research. Many thanks are also due to Professors Richard Dusansky, Thomas J. Muench and Anthoney Phillips, who are members of my dissertation committee. Discussions with Professor Phillips are especially helpful in the applications of differential topology to the model. Finally, it is my pleasure to acknowledge suggestions and comments from Dr. G. Chichilnisky, Professor M. W. Hirsch, Dr. G. Laroque and Professor J. Wolf of Harvard University during the years of 1974-1976 while I was at Harvard preparing this study.

Chapter I

INTRODUCTION

The differentiable approach to equilibrium theory originates with the works of Debreu [9], [10] and is followed up by the works of E. and H. Dierker [13] and Smale [53], [55] among others (see also [3], [14], [18] for instance). This approach allows one to directly study the structure of the set of equilibria as well as the existence problem.

From a classical viewpoint of equilibrium theory, the existence problem is simply based upon enumerating the conditions of equilibrium for each agent in the economy and counting the equations describing these equilibrium states. Unlike the mathematical tools of fixed point theorems in algebraic topology, the differentiable approach enables us to attack the equations and their solutions directly provided that the equations describing equilibrium conditions are sufficiently differentiable. Recent works on approximation theorems (for instance, see [29], [38] and [44]) give further justification to the use of the differentiable approach in economics. Once there is a general solution to an economic system, as pointed out by Debreu in [9] and [10], one should also investigate the structure of the set of equilibria. Otherwise, the explanation of equilibrium is totally indeterminate.

First, there may exist infinitely many equilibria. Also, the economic system may be unstable in the sense that a small change of economic data would lead to an entirely different set of equilibria. Therefore, it is highly desirable to have an economy for which the set of equilibria is locally unique (i.e., discrete) and stable (i.e., continuous). These properties are also needed if one wants to study the comparative statics of the system. The way of studying these equilibrium properties is provided by differential topology. In a general Walrasian equilibrium framework, Debreu [9] was the first to prove the existence and finiteness of equilibria for a space of economies with variable resources but fixed preferences for each economic agent by using Sard's theorem of differential topology. Similar results have been obtained for the case of variation of demands as well as variable resources by Dierker [14] and Fuchs [18] among others. Smale [53], [55] studied the same problem from a viewpoint of variable utility functions in a general way and does not require well defined demand functions. In this research, one considers short run or temporary equilibrium in a Walrasian setting from a differentiable viewpoint and studies the equilibrium properties for such models in which some roles of money are also examined.

The basic idea of the short-run or temporary equilibrium model is that each agent's decisions are made sequentially and may be revised as time progresses according to the information conveyed about the future environment, which is based upon the agent's current and past observations. "Loosely speaking, whereas the Arrow-Debreu analysis is essentially static, the short-run equilibrium analysis studies the dynamic features of the economy within a short time interval [56]." In a temporary equilibrium analysis, the expectations taken as data of the system link the subsequent spot markets together and play the most important role in determining the equilibrium properties with uncertain information available in the future. This idea can be traced back to the work of Hicks [32] and it is also a very much part of the Keynesian thinking. Recent contributions to temporary equilibrium theory can be found in the works of Arrow and Hahn [2] and Stigum [57], [58] among others.

For a simple case, the structure of temporary equilibrium theory reveals (indirectly) the Veblen-Scitovsky effect through the agent's price expectations. Veblen [59] argued that some commodities do have the property of demonstration of personal wealth and Scitovsky [50] concluded a result that economic agents judge the price of commodity as an index of quality, that is, price parameters influence the individual's preferences in an explicit way (see also [36]). Applying utility analysis, Dusansky and Kalman [16], [17] have shown that the derived demand of a Veblen-Scitovsky economy is usually changed non-homogeneously with respect to the proportional change in price system and initial wealth.

As a matter of fact, the basic simplified temporary equilibrium model can be easily extended to incorporate other aspects of economic activity which do not occur in an Arrow-Debreu economy. First, it is very natural to introduce a financial asset such as "money" which serves as the only store of value in a temporary equilibrium framework, and study the properties of a monetary equilibrium. This idea was adopted by Patinkin [47] in his integration of monetary and value theories. For a money economy, in general there is money illusion in the construction in addition to "judging quality by price" and "snob appeal" originated by Scitovsky and Veblen, respectively. This is a generalization of Patinkin's real balance effect (see also [16]). More recent contributions to temporary monetary equilibrium theory, especially the existence of a monetary equilibrium, can be found in the works of Grandmont [20], Grandmont and Laroque [22], [23], Grandmont and Younès [25], [26] , Hool [35], Sondermann [56] and Younès [61], among others. In these works, two assumptions on expectations were imposed. First, each agent's subjective probability distribution over future events varies continuously with respect to the current and past observations. Secondly, each agent is certain that all future prices (including future price of money) are positive and that future prices of consumption goods and asset, if any, are relatively inelastic with respect to the current and past information available in the economy. Under these assumptions, the existence of a monetary equilibrium has been established in the sense that the equilibrium price of money is positive although money has no intrinsic value for consumption purpose.

In previous discussion of temporary equilibrium models, the analysis is restricted to the "spot" markets only. It can be extended to allow the existence of future markets such that the current activities of an agent include not only the decision to make immediate consumption, but also the intention to make contracts in the more or less distant future. For a non-monetary economy with futures contracts, Green [27] considered a temporary equilibrium model in which the markets for trading current and future commodities are open at the initial date, and all future commodities are again tradable in the future. Moreover, an extension has been made in [28] to allow bankruptcy with some probability and the agents can also be endowed with preexisting contracts when the market of the current period opens. In addition to the above conditions on expectations, some degree of compatibility of expectations among agents are necessary to ensure the existence of an equilibrium with spot and futures transactions.

In this research, we formulate temporary monetary equilibrium models in a differentiable setting. Using techniques of differential topology recently introduced into the economics literature by Debreu [9], [10] and Smale [53], [55], we establish the properties of local uniqueness and stability of temporary equilibria for "almost all" money economies as well as existence for every money economy. The crucial assumptions are sufficient differentiability of the direct utility functions and expectation functions.[1] Furthermore, the conditions for the existence of temporary monetary equilibrium, as discussed earlier, contain the inelasticity of expectations in the case of pure spot markets, and together with the one which restricts the possibility of abtratige on future markets in the general case. Although these assumptions on expectations are not necessary for the study of the set of temporary monetary equilibria, we include them only for the reason of consistency of the models. We prove that the set of temporary equilibria is a finite set and depends continously on the money economy. These are new results in the literature.

In Chapter II, some basic definitions and assumptions are made and discussed for a monetary economy with spot markets. Among them, a set of classical assumptions are postulated on the future spot market which guarantee the differentiability requirement in the model. The dynamic programming approach used in this section to derive the indirect utility function originates with the works of Stigum [57], [58] and Grandmont [20]. However,

[1] Differentiability of expectations is also considered by Fuchs and Laroque [19] for a different model in which no uncertainty is considered.

they do not use a differentiable viewpoint as we do in this work. We study utility functions directly and our class of utility functions includes those which define continuously differentiable demand functions. Chapter III formulates an (infinite dimensional) space of money economies in which an element is a list of expectations, direct utility functions, money and commodity endowments. In other words, we allow changes of tastes, beliefs and endowments of all agents in the model. We prove the continuous differentiability of expected utility functions with respect to the commodity-money holding and the price system as well.[2] Moreover, a concept of "extended" monetary equilibrium is introduced, which contains (classical) monetary equilibrium. In Chapter IV the topological concept of "almost all" economies is introduced in the space of money economies. Because of the infinite dimensionality of the space of money economies, the best we can show at this point is that the set of "regular" money economies is "open and dense" in the space of all money economies with respect to an appropriate topology. Two theorems, local uniqueness and stability, are presented and proved for all regular money economies. The former can be obtained without assuming concavity of the utility functions for any agents and the latter follows from an application of the implicit function theorem. Finally, the existence of temporary monetary equilibrium is

[2] For a related result in a non-differentiable framework, see [20].

proved by demonstrating that every money economy is a continuous deformation of an economy with unique equilibrium. The technique we use is degree theory in differential topology. As an extension, in Chapter V, we introduce futures transactions in the above temporary monetary equilibrium analysis. The activities of borrowing and lending may occur by trading commodities and money deliverable in the future against present ones. The precautionary and speculative motives for money holding are obvious in the formulation. This particular chapter can be considered as an extension of Green [27] in the direction of including money and studying the existence, finiteness and stability of temporary monetary equilibria. Finally, in Chapter VI, some suggestions for further research are stated briefly.

Chapter II

A SPOT MONEY ECONOMY

We consider a framework of temporary monetary equilibrium theory with two successive periods where for each period all commodities are immediately deliverable for consumption and "money" is used as the only store of value but gives no direct utility to the agents. In such a "spot" money economy, taking into consideration future (market and individual) uncertainty, money is a link of transferring wealth between periods. The analysis is an "interior analysis" which considers only positive price systems and each agent owns at least a little of each commodity and money. Moreover, the restriction of the analysis to two periods is by no means essential, and the so-called "period" is considered as a synonym of Hicksian "week" in which markets are held on "Monday". Although it is assumed that no agent makes plans beyond one period into the future, our analysis carries over to a many but finite period planning horizon for the agent.

II(a) Basic Definitions

Suppose there are two periods t and $t+1$. For each period, there are ℓ commodities and n agents.[3] Let $P = \{z \in R^{\ell}: z \gg 0\}$[4] be the consumption space in which an element x^{ht} is a consumption bundle for agent h, $(h = 1, \ldots, n)$ at time t. We assume that all ℓ commodities are perishable and have to be consumed during one period. Let $R_+ = \{z \in R: z \geq 0\}$ and $m^{ht} \in R_+$ is the h-th agent's money holding at time t. We note that money can be stored at no cost and held between periods t and $t+1$. However, it provides no direct satisfaction from consumption to the agents. Let $S = \{(s^t, 1) \in R^{\ell+1}: s^t \gg 0\}$ be the monetary price space, where the price of money is given as unity and s^t is the price system of ℓ commodities at time t in terms of money. As agents are only interested in relative prices between money and commodities, we write

---

[3]This can be generalized in a straightforward way to a different number of commodities and agents in periods t and $t+1$, respectively.

[4]If $x, x' \in R^{\ell}$, $x \geq x'$ means $x_i \geq x'_i$ for all i; $x > x'$ means $x \geq x'$ and $x \neq x'$; $x \gg x'$ means $x_i > x'_i$ for all i.

$$\Pi = \left\{ \pi^t = (p^t, p_0^t) \in R^{\ell+1} : \ p_0^t = 1\Big/\left(\sum_{i=1}^{\ell} s_i^t + 1\right) \text{ and } \right.$$

$$\left. p_i^t = s_i^t\Big/\left(\sum_{i=1}^{\ell} s_i^t + 1\right) \text{ for every } (s^t, 1) \in S \text{ and } i = 1, \ldots, \ell \right\}$$

to be the price space. Note that only the positive price systems are considered in this pure exchange model.

At the beginning of period t, every agent h in an economy knows with certainty his initial commodity and money endowments, i.e., $(\bar{x}^{ht}, m^{ht-1}) \in P \times R_+$, where the money endowment $m^{ht-1} \in R_+$ is the cash balance carried over from the previous period. Clearly, $\Sigma_{h=1}^{n} m^{ht-1} > 0$. The h-th agent's <u>action</u> at time t is defined by a pair of commodity and money holdings, or $(x^{ht}, m^{ht}) \in P \times R_+$. A <u>consequence</u> of an action is a pair of current and future commodity consumptions denoted by $(x^{ht}, x^{ht+1}) \in P \times P$. Moreover, given $\bar{x}^{ht}$ and m^{ht-1}, the <u>wealth</u> of agent h at time t is defined by $y^{ht} = p^t \cdot \bar{x}^{ht} + p_0^t \cdot m^{ht-1}$ for each $\pi^t = (p^t, p_0^t) \in \Pi$. The <u>budget set</u> of agent h at period t is $\beta^{ht}(\pi^t, y^{ht}) = \{(x^{ht}, m^{ht}) \in P \times R_+ : \ p^t \cdot x^{ht} + p_0^t \cdot m^{ht} = y^{ht}\}$.

II(b) Expectation Functions

For each agent h, the strategy of choosing a consequence of an action at time t involves a plan $\hat{x}^{ht+1}$ (defined below) for future consumption. Intuitively, a plan of an agent must be influenced by his view of the future environment. To specify a subjective uncertainty about the future environment for each agent, one assumes that each agent forecasts future prices and commodity endowments which take the form of a probability distribution on $\Pi \times P$. In general, this forecast will depend on the current and past information available in the model. For a simple case, such an anticipation is assumed to rely upon the currently quoted price system π^t, and the sequence of past equilibrium prices which is fixed and can be neglected in a short-run analysis. More precisely, the agent's expectations can be described by a mapping $\gamma^h\colon \Pi \to \mathcal{M}(\Pi \times P)$ where the range space $\mathcal{M}(\Pi \times P)$ is the family of probability measures defined on the measure space $(\Pi \times P, \mathcal{B}(\Pi \times P))$ with $\mathcal{B}(\Pi \times P)$ denoting the Borel σ-field of $\Pi \times P$. Then, for every $B \in \mathcal{B}(\Pi \times P)$, $\gamma^h(\pi^t; B)$ is the probability of B if π^t is quoted on the t-th market. For each $\pi^t \in \Pi$, the support of a probability measure $\gamma^h(\pi^t)$, denoted supp $\gamma^h(\pi^t)$, is well defined (see [5] or [46]). It is the smallest closed set in $\Pi \times P$ with full measure. We make the following assumption:

<u>A. 1</u> For each agent h, γ^h is continuously differentiable, i.e., $\gamma^h \in C^1(\Pi, \mathcal{M}(\Pi \times P))$, and supp $\gamma^h(\pi^t)$ is contained in a fixed compact subset of $\Pi \times P$.

Roughly speaking, assumption A. 1 means that the change of the expectations of future price systems and commodity endowments are inelastic but in a continuously differentiable fashion with respect to the change of current prices.[5] Let Γ be the space of $\gamma^h: \Pi \to \mathcal{M}(\Pi \times P)$ satisfying A. 1. Γ is called the <u>space of expectations</u> for any agent.

As usual, on the space $\mathcal{M}(\Pi \times P)$, we put the topology of weak convergence of probability measures. It is well known that this is the weakest topology such that $\mu \to \int f\, d\mu$ $(\mu \in \mathcal{M}(\Pi \times P))$ is continuous for all bounded continuous real-valued functions f. Moreover, the space $\mathcal{M}(\Pi \times P)$ endowed with the topology of weak convergence is metrizable by various metrics since $\Pi \times P$ is a separable metric space (see [46], Chapter II, Theorem 6. 2). In the following, we shall use a metric which has the advantage of being defined by a norm on a linear space, so that $\mathcal{M}(\Pi \times P)$ can be given a differentiable structure of a Banach space. That is, the function space $C^1(\Pi, \mathcal{M}(\Pi \times P))$ is well defined. The metric on the space $\mathcal{M}(\Pi \times P)$ is constructed as follows: Let $BC(\Pi \times P)$ be the Banach space of bounded real-valued continuous

---

5 The idea of assuming compact support of expectations is in [20] and [61], among others. It is standard in the temporary equilibrium analysis.

functions f on $\Pi \times P$, with the norm $\|f\|_\infty = \sup\{|f(z)|: z \in \Pi \times P\}$. If $\Pi \times P$ is equipped with a metric d, a real-valued function f on $\Pi \times P$ is called Lipschitzian if

$$\|f\|_L = \sup\{|f(z) - f(z')|/d(z, z'): d(z, z') \neq 0\} < \infty .$$

Let $\|f\|_{BL} = \|f\|_L + \|f\|_\infty$, then the space of all bounded Lipschitzian functions f on $\Pi \times P$, denoted $BL(\Pi \times P)$, with the norm $\|\cdot\|_{BL}$ is a Banach space. It is clear that we can consider $\mathcal{M}(\Pi \times P)$ as a subset of the dual of $BL(\Pi \times P)$, denoted $BL^*(\Pi \times P)$, with the norm $\|\mu\|^*_{BL} = \sup\{|\int f\, d\mu|: \|f\|_{BL} \leq 1\}$. There are close relations between weak and $\|\cdot\|^*_{BL}$ convergences of probability measures. As a matter of fact, $\|\cdot\|^*_{BL}$ topology coincides with the topology of weak convergence on $\mathcal{M}(\Pi \times P)$. (This is no longer true for the space of all finite signed measures.) Therefore, the $\|\cdot\|^*_{BL}$ metric metrizes the topology of weak convergence on the space $\mathcal{M}(\Pi \times P)$.[6] In use of the $\|\cdot\|^*_{BL}$ metric, the space of expectation functions can be also written as $\Gamma = \{\gamma^h \in C^1(\Pi, BL^*(\Pi \times P)): \gamma^h(\pi^t) \geq 0, \int_{\Pi \times P} d\gamma^h(\pi^t) = 1$ and $\operatorname{supp} \gamma^h(\pi^t)$ is compact for all $\pi^t \in \Pi\}$.

For an action $(x^{ht}, m^{ht}) \in P \times R_+$ and $\pi^t \in \Pi$, analogous to the definitions of y^{ht} and $\beta^{ht}(\pi^t, y^{ht})$, the

---

[6]I am indebted to Professor R. M. Dudley of M.I.T. for pointing out to me the use of $\|\cdot\|^*_{BL}$ metric on the space $\mathcal{M}(\Pi \times P)$. See also his paper, "Convergence of Baire Measures", Studia Mathematica 27, 1966, pp. 251-268.

wealth of agent h at time t+1 is defined by

$y^{ht+1} = p^{t+1} \cdot \bar{x}^{ht+1} + p_0^{t+1} \cdot m^{ht}$ for a given future event $(\pi^{t+1}, \bar{x}^{ht+1}) \in \Pi \times P$. For convention we let $m^{ht+1} = 0$ and hence

$$\beta^{ht+1}(\pi^{t+1}, y^{ht+1}) = \{x^{ht+1} \in R_+^{\ell} : p^{t+1} \cdot x^{ht+1} = y^{ht+1}\}$$

II(c) von Neumann-Morgenstern Utility Functions

For each h, the agent's intertemporal preferences among consequences (satisfying Expected Utility Hypothesis) can be represented by a von Neumann-Morgenstern utility function $u^h : P \times P \rightarrow R$ which is a bounded and continuous real-valued function from the consequence space $P \times P$ to the real line R. We note that applying utilities as primitive concepts to describe the preference orderings may not be unique in the sense that each preference, in general, can be represented by an infinite class of utilities. However, utility functions are elements of linear function space, which provide enough structure to work on. First, we need the utility functions to be sufficiently differentiable. Fortunately, the approximation theorems proved recently by Grodal [29], Kannai [38], and Mas-Collel [44], among others, show that assuming differentiability of u^h is not unreasonable at all. Let $C^k(P \times P, R)$ be the space of k-times continuously differentiable functions from $P \times P$ to R. We assume $u^h \in C^k(P \times P, R)$, $k > 2$, for each agent h and u^h is bounded. We further assume that u^h has the property that indifference surfaces do not intersect the boundary of the consequence space (see [10]), and that u^h satisfies a monotonicity hypothesis. Formally, we have the following:

<u>A.2</u> u^h is bounded and $u^h \in C^k(P \times P, R)$ with $k > 2$, and

(i) $\overline{u^{h^{-1}}(c)} \subset P \times P$ for each $c \in R$, and

(ii) $Du^h(x^{ht}, x^{ht+1}) >> 0$ for every $(x^{ht}, x^{ht+1}) \in P \times P$

where $\overline{u^{h^{-1}}(c)}$ is the closure of indifference surface $u^{h^{-1}}(c)$ and

$$Du^h(x^{ht}, x^{ht+1}) = \left(D_{x^{ht}} u^h(x^{ht}, x^{ht+1}),\ D_{x^{ht+1}} u^h(x^{ht}, x^{ht+1})\right)$$

with

$$D_{x^{ht}} u^h(x^{ht}, x^{ht+1}) = (\partial u^h(x^{ht}, x^{ht})/\partial x_1^{ht}, \ldots, \partial u^h(x^{ht}, x^{ht+1})/\partial x_\ell^{ht})$$

and

$$D_{x^{ht+1}} u^h(x^{ht}, x^{ht+1}) = (\partial u^h(x^{ht}, x^{ht+1})/\partial x_1^{ht+1}, \ldots, \partial u^h(x^{ht}, x^{ht+1})/\partial x_\ell^{ht+1}) .$$

If one lets $D_1 u^h(x^{ht}, x^{ht+1})$ be the gradient vector of u^h with respect to the first ℓ coordinates, in general, $D_1 u^h(x^{ht}, x^{ht+1}) \neq D_{x^{ht}} u^h(x^{ht}, x^{ht+1})$ since the future consumption plan x^{ht+1} may depend on the current consumption x^{ht} as defined below.

Suppose agent h has taken an action $(x^{ht}, m^{ht}) \in P \times R_+$ at time t and faces a future environment $(\pi^{t+1}, \bar{x}^{ht+1}) \in \Pi \times P$ for each $\pi^t \in \Pi$. The decision problem of agent h in period t for period t+1 is to choose x^{ht+1} satisfying $x^{ht+1} \in \beta^{ht+1}(\pi^{t+1}, y^{ht+1})$ and that $u^h(x^{ht}, x^{ht+1})$ is maximized. Hence a plan is a correspondence defined by

$$(1) \quad \hat{x}^{ht+1}(x^{ht}, m^{ht}; \pi^{t+1}, \bar{x}^{ht+1})$$

$$= \left\{ x^{ht+1} \in P\colon u^h(x^{ht}, x^{ht+1}) \text{ is maximized and } x^{ht+1} \in \beta^{ht+1}(\pi^{t+1}, y^{ht+1}) \right\}$$

for each $(x^{ht}, m^{ht}) \in P \times R_+$ and $(\pi^{t+1}, \bar{x}^{ht+1}) \in \Pi \times P$.

Corresponding to a plan $\hat{x}^{ht+1}(x^{ht}, m^{ht}; \pi^{t+1}, \bar{x}^{ht+1})$, let

$$\hat{u}^t(x^{ht}, m^{ht}; \pi^{t+1}, \bar{x}^{ht+1}) = u^h(x^{ht}, \hat{x}^{ht+1}(x^{ht}, m^{ht}; \pi^{t+1}, \bar{x}^{ht+1}))$$

be the utility of a plan associated with an action $(x^{ht}, m^{ht}) \in P \times R_+$ and an expectation of future event $(\pi^{t+1}, \bar{x}^{ht+1}) \in \Pi \times P$. In order to preserve enough differentiability in the model, a classical assumption on the future market is made for each agent h. That is,

<u>A. 3</u> $D^2_{x^{ht+1}} u^h(x^{ht}, x^{ht+1})$ is negative definite on the space

$$\left\{\mu \in R^{\ell} : D_{x^{ht+1}} u^h(x^{ht}, x^{ht+1}) \cdot \mu = 0\right\}$$

for every $(x^{ht}, x^{ht+1}) \in P \times P$,

where $D^2_{x^{ht+1}} u^h(x^{ht}, x^{ht+1})$ is the bilinear symmetric form of $u^h(x^{ht}, x^{ht+1})$ with respect to x^{ht+1}. A. 3 means the "Hessian" is negative definite for small disturbance along the contour of u^h with respect to future consumption. This is not a concavity hypothesis of u^h on the consequence space usually assumed in the literature. Let $\mathcal{U}$ be the collection of $u^h : P \times P \to R$ satisfying A. 2 and A. 3. $\mathcal{U}$ is called the space of <u>direct utility functions</u> from $P \times P$ to R for every agent h. For a classical case of $\mathcal{U}$, we also consider a subspace of direct utility functions denoted by $\mathcal{U}_0$ i. e.,

$$\mathcal{U}_0 = \left\{u^h \in \mathcal{U} : D^2 u^h(x^{ht}, x^{ht+1}) \text{ is negative definite on the space } \{\xi \in R^{2\ell} : Du^h(x^{ht}, x^{ht+1}) \cdot \xi = 0\} \text{ for every } (x^{ht}, x^{ht+1}) \in P \times P\right\}$$

As we discussed earlier, for any $u^h \in \mathcal{U}$ and $\gamma^h \in \Gamma$, there is a plan $\hat{x}^{ht+1}$ defined by (1) which is an outcome of constrained utility maximization of period $t+1$ conditional to a given action and an expectation of future event. We have the following

PROPOSITION 1. $\hat{x}^{ht+1} \in C^{k-1}(P \times R_+ \times \Pi \times P, P)$ with $k > 2$, where $\hat{x}^{ht+1}$ is defined by (1) for each $u^h \in \mathscr{U}$ and $\gamma^h \in \Gamma$.

Proof. (See also [39], [10], and [53].) By Definition (1) and assumption A. 3, given an action $(x^{ht}, m^{ht}) \in P \times R_+$ and a future event $(\pi^{t+1}, \bar{x}^{ht+1}) \in \Pi \times P$, the set

$$\hat{x}^{ht+1}(x^{ht}, m^{ht}; \pi^{t+1}, \bar{x}^{ht+1})$$

$$= \Big\{ x^{ht+1} \in P\colon D_{x^{ht+1}} u^h(x^{ht}, x^{ht+1}) = \lambda^h \cdot p^{t+1} \text{ and}$$

$$p^{t+1} \cdot x^{ht+1} = p^{t+1} \cdot \bar{x}^{ht+1} + p_0^{t+1} \cdot m^{ht} \Big\},$$

where λ^h is the Lagrangian Multiplier which can be substituted by the value

$$\left| D_{x^{ht+1}} u^h(x^{ht}, x^{ht+1}) \right| \Big/ 1 - p_0^{t+1}$$

where

$$\left| D_{x^{ht+1}} u^h(x^{ht}, x^{ht+1}) \right| = \sum_{i=1}^{\ell} \partial u^h(x^{ht}, x^{ht+1}) / \partial x_i^{ht+1}$$

A. 2(ii) shows that $\lambda^h > 0$. Thus we write

$$\hat{x}^{ht+1}(x^{ht}, m^{ht}; \pi^{t+1}, \bar{x}^{ht+1})$$

$$= \Big\{ x^{ht+1} \in P:\ D_{x^{ht+1}} u^h(x^{ht}, x^{ht+1}) = \left| D_{x^{ht+1}} u^h(x^{ht}, x^{ht+1}) \right| \cdot \frac{p^{t+1}}{1-p_0^{t+1}}$$

$$\text{and } p^{t+1} \cdot x^{ht+1} = p^{t+1} \cdot \bar{x}^{ht+1} + p_0^{t+1} \cdot m^{ht} \Big\}$$

For a given $u^h \in \mathscr{U}$, we define

$$\alpha^h_{u^h}(x^{ht+1} \mid x^{ht}, m^{ht}; \pi^{t+1}, \bar{x}^{ht+1})$$

$$= \Big(D_{x^{ht+1}} u^h(x^{ht}, x^{ht+1}) - \left| D_{x^{ht+1}} u^h(x^{ht}, x^{ht+1}) \right| \cdot \frac{p^{t+1}}{1-p_0^{t+1}},$$

$$p^{t+1} \cdot \bar{x}^{ht+1} + p_0^{t+1} \cdot m^{ht} - p^{t+1} \cdot x^{ht+1} \Big)$$

Obviously, $\alpha^h_{u^h} \in C^{k-1}(P \times P \times R_+ \times \Pi \times P,\ I \times R)$, where $I = \{ z \in R^{\ell}:\ \Sigma_{i=1}^{\ell} z_i = 0 \}$. Furthermore,

$$\alpha^h_{u^h}(\cdot \mid x^{ht}, m^{ht}; \pi^{t+1}, \bar{x}^{ht+1})^{-1}(0) = \hat{x}^{ht+1}(x^{ht}, m^{ht}; \pi^{t+1}, \bar{x}^{ht+1})$$

for each $u^h \in \mathscr{U}$ and $(x^{ht}, m^{ht}; \pi^{t+1}, \bar{x}^{ht+1}) \in P \times R_+ \times \Pi \times P$.

We claim that the derivative matrix of $\alpha^h_{u^h}(x^{ht+1} \mid x^{ht}, m^{ht}; \pi^{t+1}, \bar{x}^{ht+1})$ with respect to x^{ht+1}, denoted by

$$D_{x^{ht+1}} \alpha^h_{u^h}(x^{ht+1} \mid x^{ht}, m^{ht}; \pi^{t+1}, \bar{x}^{ht+1}) \quad ,$$

has rank ℓ for each $u^h \in \mathcal{U}$ and $(x^{ht}, m^{ht}; \pi^{t+1}, \bar{x}^{ht+1}) \in P \times R_+ \times \Pi \times P$.

This follows from A. 3 and the fact that

$$\det \left(\begin{array}{c|c} D_{x^{ht+1}} u^h(x^{ht}, x^{ht+1}) & \dfrac{-p^{t+1}}{1 - p_0^{t+1}} \\ \hline \dfrac{-p^{t+1}}{1 - p_0^{t+1}} & 0 \end{array} \right) \neq 0$$

(Note that we use the same vector notation for the column and row vectors.) And

$$\det \left(\begin{array}{c|c} D_{x^{ht+1}} u^h(x^{ht}, x^{ht+1}) & \dfrac{-p^{t+1}}{1 - p_0^{t+1}} \\ \hline \dfrac{-p^{t+1}}{1 - p_0^{t+1}} & 0 \end{array} \right)$$

$$= \det \left(D_{x^{ht+1}} \alpha^h_{u^h}(x^{ht+1} \mid x^{ht}, m^{ht}; \pi^{t+1}, \bar{x}^{ht+1}) \begin{array}{|c} -p^{t+1}/1-p_0^{t+1} \\ 0 \end{array} \right)$$

$$= \det D_{x^{ht+1}} \tilde{\alpha}^h_{u^h}(x^{ht+1} \mid x^{ht}, m^{ht}; \pi^{t+1}, \bar{x}^{ht+1})$$

where $D_{x^{ht+1}} \tilde{\alpha}^h_{u^h}(x^{ht+1} \mid x^{ht}, m^{ht}; \pi^{t+1}, \bar{x}^{ht+1})$ is exactly the matrix $D_{x^{ht+1}} \alpha^h_{u^h}(x^{ht+1} \mid x^{ht}, m^{ht}; \pi^{t+1}, \bar{x}^{ht+1})$ with the ℓ-th row deleted. From the inverse function theorem and A. 3, $\alpha^h_{u^h}(\cdot \mid x^{ht}, m^{ht}; \pi^{t+1}, \bar{x}^{ht+1})$ is a local C^1 diffeomorphism for any $(x^{ht}, m^{ht}; \pi^{t+1}, \bar{x}^{ht+1}) \in P \times R_+ \times \Pi \times P$. Let

$$\alpha^h_{u^h}(x^{ht+1} \mid x^{ht}, m^{ht}; \pi^{t+1}, \bar{x}^{ht+1}) = 0 .$$

By the implicit function theorem, there is a unique C^{k-1} function f from a neighborhood of $(x^{ht}, m^{ht}; \pi^{t+1}, \bar{x}^{ht+1})$ in $P \times R_+ \times \Pi \times P$ into P with $k > 2$ such that

$$f(x^{ht}, m^{ht}; \pi^{t+1}, \bar{x}^{ht+1}) = x^{ht+1}$$

and

$$\alpha^h_{u^h}\left(f(x^{ht'}, m^{ht'}; \pi^{t+1'}, \bar{x}^{ht+1'}) \mid x^{ht'}, m^{ht'}; \pi^{t+1'}, \bar{x}^{ht+1'}\right) = 0$$

for any $(x^{ht'}, m^{ht'}; \pi^{t+1'}, \bar{x}^{ht+1'})$ in this neighborhood. Since f is unique, set $f = \hat{x}^{ht+1}$. Q. E. D.

II(d) Expected Utility Functions

For a given $u^h \in \mathcal{U}$ and $\gamma^h \in \Gamma$, if π^t is the price system at time t, the agent's expected utility function of an action (x^{ht}, m^{ht}) is defined by

$$(2) \qquad v^h(x^{ht}, m^{ht}, \pi^t; \gamma^h, u^h) = \int_{\Pi \times P} \hat{u}^h(x^{ht}, m^{ht}; \cdot, \cdot)\, d\gamma^h(\pi^t; \cdot, \cdot)$$

We observe that the expected utility function v^h defined by (2) depends on money m^{ht} and current price π^t explicitly, which reflects a "generalized real balance effect" (see, for example, [16]). It is important to notice that, in general, v^h is not homogeneous of any degree in m^{ht} and π^t; thus we allow for the possibility of "money illusion" in the expected utility function v^h for every agent h (see, for example, [17] and [10]). We also express in (2) that the expected utility function depends on the economic exogenous data $(\gamma^h, u^h) \in \Gamma \times \mathcal{U}$. Hence v^h is allowed to vary in the product space $\Gamma \times \mathcal{U}$.[7] This means that changes of views or beliefs of the future environment and changes in tastes are capable of influending the present situation which is represented by the expected utility function v^h. We have the following:

PROPOSITION 2. <u>For each agent</u> h, $v^h(\cdot, \cdot, \cdot; \gamma^h, u^h)$ <u>is continuously differentiable</u>, <u>i.e.</u>, $v^h(\cdot, \cdot, \cdot; \gamma^h, u^h) \in C^1(P \times R_+ \times \Pi, R)$ <u>for each</u> $\gamma^h \in \Gamma$ <u>and</u> $u^h \in \mathcal{U}$. <u>In</u>

---

[7] For related works, see, for example [20], which considers a similar model with a fixed u^h and γ^h for each agent h and proves the existence of an equilibrium using a standard fixed point argument, and also [6] which holds u^h fixed and allows γ^h to vary to study the continuity of temporary equilibrium in a non-differentiable framework.

<u>particular,</u> $v^h(\cdot, \cdot, \pi^t; \gamma^h, u^h) \in C^k(P \times R_+, R)$ <u>with</u> $k > 2$ <u>for every</u> $\pi^t \in \Pi$.

<u>Proof.</u> First, by Proposition 1, $\hat{x}^{ht+1} \in C^{k-1}(P \times R_+ \times \Pi \times P, P)$ defined by (1) with $k > 2$. Hence, the utility function $\hat{u}^h \in C^{k-1}(P \times R_+ \times \Pi \times P, R)$. According to (2), v^h is clearly well defined, and hence, $v^h(\cdot, \cdot, \pi^t; \gamma^h, u^h) \in C^{k-1}(P \times R_+, R)$ with $k > 2$ for each $\pi^t \in \Pi$, $\gamma^h \in \Gamma$ and $u^h \in \mathcal{U}$. Moreover, the assumption A. 1 implies that $v^h(\cdot, \cdot, \cdot; \gamma^h, u^h) \in C^1(P \times R_+ \times \Pi, R)$ for each $\gamma^h \in \Gamma$ and $u^h \in \mathcal{U}$. Q. E. D.

For notational convenience, let

$$D_1 v^h(x^{ht}, m^{ht}, \pi^t; \gamma^h, u^h)$$

$$= (\partial v^h(x^{ht}, m^{ht}, \pi^t; \gamma^h, u^h)/\partial x_1^{ht}, \ldots, \partial v^h(x^{ht}, m^{ht}, \pi^t; \gamma^h, u^h)/\partial x_\ell^{ht}),$$

$$D_2 v^h(x^{ht}, m^{ht}, \pi^t; \gamma^h, u^h) = \partial v^h(x^{ht}, m^{ht}, \pi^t; \gamma^h, u^h)/\partial m^{ht},$$

and

$$D_a v^h(x^{ht}, m^{ht}, \pi^t; \gamma^h, u^h)$$

$$= (D_1 v^h(x^{ht}, m^{ht}, \pi^t; \gamma^h, u^h), D_2 v^h(x^{ht}, m^{ht}, \pi^t; \gamma^h, u^h)).$$

PROPOSITION 3. $\overline{v^h(\cdot, m^{ht}, \pi^t; \gamma^h, u^h)^{-1}(c)} \subset P$ *for every* $\gamma^h \in \Gamma$, $u^h \in \mathscr{U}$, $(m^{ht}, \pi^t) \in R_+ \times \Pi$, and $c \in R$. *Moreover,*

$$D_a v^h(x^{ht}, m^{ht}, \pi^t; \gamma^h, u^h)$$

$$= \int_{\Pi \times P} D_a \hat{u}^h(x^{ht}, m^{ht}; \cdot, \cdot)\, d\gamma^h(\pi^t; \cdot, \cdot)$$

$$= \left(\int_{\Pi \times P} D_{x^{ht}} \hat{u}^h(x^{ht}, m^{ht}; \cdot, \cdot)\, d\gamma^h(\pi^t; \cdot, \cdot), \right.$$

$$\left. \int_{\Pi \times P} D_{m^{ht}} \hat{u}^h(x^{ht}, m^{ht}; \cdot, \cdot)\, d\gamma^h(\pi^t; \cdot, \cdot) \right) \gg 0$$

for each $(x^{ht}, m^{ht}, \pi^t) \in P \times R_+ \times \Pi$.

Proof. The first part of the Proposition 3 is straightforward. It is clear that

$$D_1 v^h(x^{ht}, m^{ht}, \pi^t; \gamma^h, u^h) = \int_{\Pi \times P} D_{x^{ht}} \hat{u}^h(x^{ht}, m^{ht}; \cdot, \cdot)\, d\gamma^h(\pi^t; \cdot, \cdot)$$

and

$$D_2 v^h(x^{ht}, m^{ht}, \pi^t; \gamma^h, u^h) = \int_{\Pi \times P} D_{m^{ht}} \hat{u}^h(x^{ht}, m^{ht}; \cdot, \cdot)\, d\gamma^h(\pi^t; \cdot, \cdot)$$

for each $u^h \in \mathscr{U}$ and $\gamma^h \in \Gamma$ by the "Leibniz rule" for the derivative of an integral, since supp $\gamma^h(\pi^t)$ is compact for each $\pi^t \in \Pi$ (see A. 1). Hence $D_1 v^h(x^{ht}, m^{ht}, \pi^t; \gamma^h, u^h) \gg 0$ for each $(x^{ht}, m^{ht}, \pi^t) \in P \times R_+ \times \Pi$ follows from A. 2(ii). By definition (1) of a plan $\hat{x}^{ht+1}$, one has $p^{t+1} \cdot x^{ht+1} = p^{t+1} \cdot \bar{x}^{ht+1} + p_0^{t+1} \cdot m^{ht}$ if $x^{ht+1} \in \hat{x}^{ht+1}(x^{ht}, m^{ht}; \pi^{t+1}, \bar{x}^{ht+1})$ for an action (x^{ht}, m^{ht}) and a future event $(\pi^{t+1}, \bar{x}^{ht+1}) \in \Pi \times P$. Since

$$D_{m^{ht}} \hat{u}^h(x^{ht}, m^{ht}; \pi^{t+1}, \bar{x}^{ht+1})$$

$$= D_{x^{ht+1}} u^h(x^{ht}, \hat{x}^{ht+1}(x^{ht}, m^{ht}; \pi^{t+1}, \bar{x}^{ht+1}))$$

$$\cdot D_{m^{ht}} \hat{x}^{ht+1}(x^{ht}, m^{ht}; \pi^{t+1}, \bar{x}^{ht+1})$$

$$= \sum_{i=1}^{\ell} (\partial u^h(x^{ht}, \hat{x}^{ht+1}(x^{ht}, m^{ht}; \pi^{t+1}, \bar{x}^{ht+1}))/\partial x_i^{ht+1})$$

$$\cdot (p_0^{t+1}/p_i^{t+1}) ,$$

by A. 2(ii) and the fact that $\pi^{t+1} = (p^{t+1}, p_0^{t+1}) \gg 0$, it is easy to see $D_2 v^h(x^{ht}, m^{ht}, \pi^t; \gamma^h, u^h) > 0$. Q. E. D.

In view of Proposition 3, we establish the desirability of money, although it has no intrinsic value in terms of von Neumann-Morgenstern utility. Finally, the existence of a classical expected utility function is presented in the following (see [20] for a proof of the nondifferentiable case).

PROPOSITION 4. Given $\pi^t \in \Pi$, if v^h is induced by $u^h \in \mathcal{U}_0$ and $\gamma^h \in \Gamma$, $v^h(\cdot, \cdot, \pi^t; \gamma^h, u^h)$ is a differentiably concave C^{k-1} function from $P \times R_+$ to R with $k > 2$. That is, there exist $\theta \in R^{\ell+1}$ such that the matrix $D_a^2 v^h(x^{ht}, m^{ht}, \pi^t; \gamma^h, u^h)$ is negative definite on the space

$$\{\theta \in R^{\ell+1} : D_a v^h(x^{ht}, m^{ht}, \pi^t; \gamma^h, u^h) \cdot \theta = 0\}$$

for every action $(x^{ht}, m^{ht}) \in P \times R_+$.

Proof. We need to show $\theta \cdot D_a^2 v^h(x^{ht}, m^{ht}, \pi^t; \gamma^h, u^h) \cdot \theta < 0$ for any $\theta \neq 0$ and $D_a v^h(x^{ht}, m^{ht}, \pi^t; \gamma^h, u^h) \cdot \theta = 0$ (note that we use the same vector notation for the column and row vectors), provided such θ exists. Write $\theta = (\theta_x, \theta_m) \in R^{\ell} \times R$, then

$$D_a \hat{u}^h(x^{ht}, m^{ht}; \pi^{t+1}, \bar{x}^{ht+1}) \cdot \theta$$

$$= \left(D_{x^{ht}} \hat{u}^h(x^{ht}, m^{ht}; \pi^{t+1}, \bar{x}^{ht+1}), D_{m^{ht}} \hat{u}^h(x^{ht}, m^{ht}; \pi^{t+1}, \bar{x}^{ht+1})\right) \cdot (\theta_x, \theta_m)$$

$$= D_{x^{ht}} u^h(x^{ht}, \hat{x}^{ht+1}(x^{ht}, m^{ht}; \pi^{t+1}, \bar{x}^{ht+1})) \cdot \theta_x +$$

$$+ D_{x^{ht+1}} u^h(x^{ht}, \hat{x}^{ht+1}(x^{ht}, m^{ht}; \pi^{t+1}, \bar{x}^{ht+1}))$$

$$\cdot D_{m^{ht}} \hat{x}^{ht+1}(x^{ht}, m^{ht}; \pi^{t+1}, \bar{x}^{ht+1}) \cdot \theta_m$$

Since $u^h \in \mathcal{U}_0$, $D^2u^h(x^{ht}, x^{ht+1})$ is negative definite on the space $\{\xi = (\xi_1, \xi_2) \in R^{2\ell}: Du^h(x^{ht}, x^{ht+1}) \cdot \xi = 0\}$ for every $(x^{ht}, x^{ht+1}) \in P \times P$. Let $\theta_x = \xi_1$ and $D_{m^{ht}} \hat{x}^{ht+1}(x^{ht}, m^{ht}; \pi^{t+1}, \bar{x}^{ht+1}) \cdot \theta_m = \xi_2$, we have $D_a \hat{u}^h(x^{ht}, m^{ht}; \pi^{t+1}, \bar{x}^{ht+1}) \cdot \theta = 0$. In the following, for notational simplicity, we denote $\hat{u}^h$ and $\hat{x}^{ht+1}$ for $\hat{u}^h(x^{ht}, m^{ht}; \pi^{t+1}, \bar{x}^{ht+1})$ and $\hat{x}^{ht+1}(x^{ht}, m^{ht}; \pi^{t+1}, \bar{x}^{ht+1})$, respectively. Moreover, $\hat{u}^h = u^h(x^{ht}, \hat{x}^{ht+1})$.

Now,

$$\theta \cdot D_a^2 \hat{u}^h \cdot \theta = \theta_x \cdot D^2_{x^{ht}x^{ht}} \hat{u}^h \cdot \theta_x + 2\theta_x \cdot D^2_{x^{ht}m^{ht}} \hat{u}^h \cdot \theta_m + \theta_m D^2_{m^{ht}m^{ht}} \hat{u}^h \cdot \theta_m$$

$$= \theta_x \cdot D^2_{x^{ht}x^{ht}} u^h(x^{ht}, \hat{x}^{ht+1}) \cdot \theta_x$$

$$+ 2\theta_x \cdot D^2_{x^{ht}x^{ht+1}} u^h(x^{ht}, \hat{x}^{ht+1}) \cdot D_{m^{ht}} \hat{x}^{ht+1} \cdot \theta_m$$

$$+ \theta_x \cdot D_{x^{ht+1}} u^h(x^{ht}, \hat{x}^{ht+1}) \cdot D^2_{x^{ht}m^{ht}} \hat{x}^{ht+1} \cdot$$

$$+ \theta_m \cdot D_{m^{ht}} \hat{x}^{ht+1} \cdot D^2_{x^{ht+1}x^{ht+1}} u^h(x^{ht}, \hat{x}^{ht+1}) \cdot D_{m^{ht}} \hat{x}^{ht+1} \cdot \theta_m +$$

$$+ \theta_m \cdot D_{x^{ht+1}} u^h(x^{ht}, \hat{x}^{ht+1}) \cdot D^2_{m^{ht}m^{ht}} \hat{x}^{ht+1}$$

$$= \xi_1 \cdot D^2_{x^{ht}x^{ht}} u^h(x^{ht}, \hat{x}^{ht+1}) \cdot \xi_1 + 2\xi_1 \cdot D^2_{x^{ht}x^{ht+1}} u^h(x^{ht}, \hat{x}^{ht+1}) \cdot \xi_2$$

$$+ \xi_2 \cdot D^2_{x^{ht+1}x^{ht+1}} u^h(x^{ht}, \hat{x}^{ht+1}) \cdot \xi_2$$

since we choose $\theta_x = \xi_1$ and $D_{m^{ht}} \hat{x}^{ht+1} \cdot \theta_m = \xi_2$. Thus, $\theta \cdot D^2_a \hat{u}^h \cdot \theta < 0$ for any $\theta \neq 0$ and $D_a \hat{u}^h \cdot \theta = 0$. Hence, $D^2_a v^h(x^{ht}, m^{ht}, \pi^t; \gamma^h, u^h)$ is negative definite on the space $\{\theta \in R^{\ell+1}: D_a v^h(x^{ht}, m^{ht}, \pi^t; \gamma^h, u^h) \cdot \theta = 0\}$ for every $(x^{ht}, m^{ht}) \in P \times R_+$ and $\pi^t \in \Pi$.

Q.E.D.

Now, the agent's decision problem in period t can be stated as follows: for each $u^h \in \mathcal{U}$ and $\gamma^h \in \Gamma$, if π^t is quoted in period t, the agent facing a future environment $(\pi^{t+1}, \bar{x}^{ht+1})$ will choose an action (x^{ht}, m^{ht}) to optimize the expected utility v^h over the budget set $\beta^{ht}(\pi^t, y^{ht})$ provided that the plan $\hat{x}^{ht+1}(x^{ht}, m^{ht}; \pi^{t+1}, \bar{x}^{ht+1})$ is realized according to (1). In what follows, we shall omit the time superscripts t and t+1, and replace m^{ht+1} by $\bar{m}^h$.

Chapter III

THE SPACE OF MONEY ECONOMIES

We are now able to define a space of money economies at period t. First, for each $u^h \in \mathcal{U}$ and $\gamma^h \in \Gamma$ we have an expected utility function v^h defined by (2). Hence the function spaces Γ and $\mathcal{U}$ are important ingredients in the definition of the space of money economies. Moreover, money and commodity endowments in period t are also allowed to vary in the space $P \times R_+$ in addition to varying the γ^h's and u^h's for every agent h. In particular, we do not restrict our analysis to a fixed amount of money supply in the model. Therefore, at time t, all economic characteristics of the model are completely specified by the product space $(\Gamma \times \mathcal{U} \times P \times R_+)^n$. Denote the space of money economies at time t by $\mathcal{E} = (\Gamma \times \mathcal{U} \times P \times R_+)^n$, and a money economy $E = (\gamma, u, \bar{x}, \bar{m})$ is an element of $\mathcal{E}$ where $\gamma = (\gamma^1, \ldots, \gamma^n)$, $u = (u^1, \ldots, u^n)$, $\bar{x} = (\bar{x}^1, \ldots, \bar{x}^n)$ and $\bar{m} = (\bar{m}^1, \ldots, \bar{m}^n)$. In other words, $E \in \mathcal{E}$ is a list of expectations, direct utility functions, commodity and money endowments at time t for all agents in the model. In particular, $\mathcal{E}_0 = (\Gamma \times \mathcal{U}_0 \times P \times R_+)^n$ is a space of classical money economies. Clearly, $\mathcal{E}$ and $\mathcal{E}_0$ are infinite-dimensional spaces, since for each agent h the utility function u^h and expectation function γ^h are allowed to vary in $\mathcal{U}$ and Γ, respectively. Hence, in addition to allowing commodity and money endowments to vary, we also allow for changes of tastes and beliefs. This extends Debreu's [9] case (in the general Walrasian equilibrium model) where the space of economies is naturally a finite dimensional Euclidean space, since only initial endowments are allowed to vary.[8]

III(a) Mathematical Preliminaries

This section, which is self contained, defines some of the mathematical concepts of the function space of k-times continuously differentiable maps from an open set U of R^m to R^n, denoted by $C^k(U, R^n)$. Let $L(R^m, R^n)$ be the space of continuous linear maps from R^m to R^n and $L^k(R^m, R^n)$ the space of continuous k-multilinear maps from R^m to R^n, i.e., $L^0(R^m, R^n) = R^n$, $L^1(R^m, R^n) = L(R^m, L^0(R^m, R^n)) = L(R^m, R^n)$ and $L^k(R^m, R^n) = L(R^m, L^{k-1}(R^m, R^n))$. Then f is said to be differentiable at $x \in U$ if $Df(x) \in L(R^m, R^n)$ such that $Df(x)(h) = \lim_{t\to 0} (f(x+th) - f(x))/t$ for any $h \in R^m$. $Df(x)$ is called the derivative of f at x. $f \in C^1(U, R^n)$ if and

---

[8]Recently, in the Walrasian general equilibrium framework, E. and H. Dierker [13] and Smale [53] extended Debreu's [9] case to the cases of allowing demand functions and utility functions to vary, respectively. This has not been done for the temporary equilibrium model with money and uncertainty. In addition, to vary money supply amounts a change of characteristics of the

only if f is differentiable at each $x \in U$ and the derivative map $Df: U \to L(R^m, R^n)$ is continuous. In general, $f \in C^k(U, R^n)$ if and only if $D^{k-1}f$ is differentiable at each $x \in U$ and the map $D^k f: U \to L^k(R^m, R^n)$ is continuous. In fact, if $f \in C^k(U, R^n)$ then $D^k f(x)$ is a symmetric k-multilinear map in $L^k(R^m, R^n)$ for $x \in U$ (see [15]). For each $f \in C^k(U, R^n)$, we define the norm of $C^k(U, R^n)$ to be

$$\|f\| = \sup \left\{ \|D^\alpha f(x)\| : x \in U, \quad \alpha = 0, 1, 2, \ldots, k \right\}$$

where $\|D^\alpha f(x)\|$ is the chosen norm of $L^\alpha(R^m, R^n)$ at $x \in U \subset R^m$. In particular, $\|D^0 f(x)\|$ means $|f(x)|$. Given $f \in C^k(U, R^n)$, and K a compact subset of U in R^m and $\epsilon > 0$, let $\eta(f, K, \epsilon)$ be the set of C^k maps $g: U \to R^n$ such that

$$\|D^\alpha f(x) - D^\alpha g(x)\| < \epsilon$$

for all $x \in K$, $\alpha = 0, 1, 2, \ldots, k$. This means that the functions f and g, together with their first k derivatives, are within ϵ distance at each point of the compact set K. The sets $\eta(f, K, \epsilon)$ form a base for what is called the C^k compact-open topology on $C^k(U, R^n)$. The C^k compact-open topology on $C^k(U, R^n)$ controls the "closeness" of maps only over compact subsets of U, and it is most useful when the domain space U is locally

---

money economy. Since our results do not depend on any restrictions of changes of initial commodity and money endowment, it is not necessary to assume that money supply $\Sigma_{h=1}^{n} m^{h}$ t-lis a constant even in the short-run.

compact. This is the weakest topology we shall consider for a definition of neighboring money economies. However, since the C^k compact-open topology does not control the behavior of a map "at infinity" very well, it is no good for dealing with "generic" properties on $C^k(U, R^n)$. Let $\delta(f, \epsilon)$ be the set of C^k maps $g: U \to R^n$ such that

$$\|D^\alpha f(x) - D^\alpha g(x)\| < \epsilon(x)$$

for all $x \in U$, $\alpha = 0, 1, 2, \ldots, k$ and $\epsilon: U \to R$ is a positive continuous mapping. These sets generate a base for the Whitney C^k topology on $C^k(U, R^n)$. If the domain space is compact, the C^k compact-open topology coincides with the Whitney C^k topology. Note that a space together with the Whitney C^k topology may not be metrizable, but in many cases it is a Baire space, that is, the intersection of a countable family of dense open sets is dense. In particular, $C^k(U, R^n)$ with the Whitney C^k topology is a Baire space. For a discussion of C^k compact-open topology and Whitney C^k topology, see [34], Chapter II, [48], and [53].

Finally, for those notions of differential topology not explained herein, the reader is referred to Abraham and Robbin [1], Hirsch [34], and Milnor [45]. Although in this section we look at only the function space defined on finite dimensional Euclidean spaces, it is also applicable to the case of Banach spaces. See [1] for a reference.

III(b) Topological Structure of the Space of Money Economies

In what follows we need an appropriate topology defined on the space of money economies $\mathscr{E}$. Since $\mathscr{E}$ is an n-fold product of the space of expectations, the space of direct utilities and the space of all endowments, the topological structure of $\mathscr{E}$ can be considered separately for each of its components. That is, the topology of $\mathscr{E}$ is exactly the n-fold product of the appropriate topologies defined on Γ, $\mathscr{U}$, P and R_+, respectively. First, we shall impose a topology on the function space $\mathscr{U} \subset C^k(P \times P, R)$ with a closeness property up to the k-th derivatives. Intuitively, the first topology which comes to mind for $\mathscr{U}$ is the one which is induced by the C^k compact-open topology on $C^k(P \times P, R)$. It is metrizable and the evaluation map defined by a map from $\mathscr{U} \times P \times P$ into R restricted to the compact subset of $P \times P$ is class C^k (see, for instance, [1], page 25 and page 31). Because $P \times P$ is clearly not compact, the induced C^k compact-open topology does not control the behavior of the map u^h "at infinity" very well. For this purpose, the Whitney C^k topology on $C^k(P \times P, R)$ is useful, which is certainly stronger than the C^k compact-open topology and the concept of convergence is even stronger than the C^k uniform convergence. We note that the space $\mathscr{U}$ together with the induced Whitney C^k topology is no longer a topological vector space. Similarly, the topology on Γ can be defined by imposing the C^1 compact-open topology or the Whitney C^1 topology on $C^1(\Pi, \mathcal{M}(\Pi \times P))$ where $\mathcal{M}(\Pi \times P)$ endowed with the topology of weak convergence is metrizable by $\| \cdot \|^*_{BL}$ metric.

As noted in the beginning of this section, toward studying the "generic" properties of monetary equilibrium, we can now precisely define the "strong" topology of the space $\mathcal{E}$ by the n-fold product of the induced Whitney C^1 topology on Γ (provided the space of probability measures $\mathcal{M}(\Pi \times P)$ is endowed with the topology of weak convergence), the induced Whitney C^k topology on $\mathcal{U}$, and the induced usual topologies on P and R_+, respectively. In proving the existence theorem (Chapter IV, Section IV(c)), the "weak" topology of $\mathcal{E}$ is then defined by replacing the Whitney C^1 topology and Whitney C^k topology by the C^1 compact-open topology and C^k compact-open topology on $C^1(\Pi, \mathcal{M}(\Pi \times P))$ and $C^k(P \times P, R)$, respectively.

III(c) <u>Two Concepts of Equilibrium</u>

As usual, for every money economy $E = (\gamma, u, \bar{x}, \bar{m}) \in \mathcal{E}$, a temporary monetary equilibrium at the current period is a triple (x, m, π) with $\Sigma^n_{h=1} x^h = \Sigma^n_{h=1} \bar{x}^h$ and $\Sigma^n_{h=1} m^h = \Sigma^n_{h=1} \bar{m}^h$, satisfying $(x^h, m^h) \in \beta^h(\pi, y^h)$ and that $v^h(x^h, m^h, \pi; \gamma^h, u^h)$

defined by (2) is maximized for every agent h. We recall that if $f: U \to R^n$ is class C^1, a point $x \in U \subset R^m$ is a regular point of f if $Df(x): R^m \to R^n$ is surjective with $y = f(x)$ where $Df(x) \in L(R^m, R^n)$ represents the derivative of the map f computed at x. If $Df(x)$ is not surjective, x is a critical point of f. y is called a regular value if every $x \in f^{-1}(y)$ is a regular point. y is a critical value if at least one $x \in f^{-1}(y)$ is a critical point. For any agent h, the Lagrangian condition for (x^h, m^h) to be a critical point of $v^h(\cdot, \cdot, \pi; \gamma^h, u^h)$ subject to $(x^h, m^h) \in \beta^h(\pi, y^h)$ can be written as $D_a v^h(x^h, m^h, \pi; \gamma^h, u^h) = \lambda^h \cdot \pi$, where λ^h is the Lagrangian Multiplier. It is obvious that λ^h depends upon the economic characteristics in the model. To avoid λ^h in the following analysis, we set λ^h at its equilibrium situation for every h, i.e.,

$$\lambda^h = |D_a v^h(x^h, m^h, \pi; \gamma^h, u^h)|$$

where

$$|D_a v^h(x^h, m^h, \pi; \gamma^h, u^h)| = \sum_{i=1}^{\ell} \partial v^h(x^h, m^h, \pi; \gamma^h, u^h)/\partial x_i^h + \partial v^h(x^h, m^h, \pi; \gamma^h, u^h)/\partial m^h$$

It is obvious that $\lambda^h > 0$ by Proposition 3.

Formally, we define the set of temporary monetary equilibria for $E \in \mathscr{E}$ as

$$W(E) = \left\{ (x,m,\pi) \in P^n \times R_+^n \times \Pi : v^h(x^h, m^h, \pi; \gamma^h, u^h) \text{ is maximized,} \right.$$

$$(3) \qquad p \cdot x^h + p_0 \cdot m^h = p \cdot \bar{x}^h + p_0 \cdot \bar{m}^h, \quad h = 1, \ldots, n, \quad \text{and}$$

$$\left. \sum_{h=1}^{n} x^h = \sum_{h=1}^{n} \bar{x}^h , \qquad \sum_{h=1}^{n} m^h = \sum_{h=1}^{n} \bar{m}^h \right\}$$

and the set of extended temporary monetary equilibria for $E \in \mathscr{E}$ as

$$\Phi(E) = \left\{ (x,m,\pi) \in P^n \times R_+^n \times \Pi : D_a v^h(x^h, m^h, \pi; \gamma^h, u^h) \right.$$

$$= |D_a v^h(x^h, m^h, \pi; \gamma^h, u^h)| \cdot \pi,$$

$$(4) \qquad p \cdot x^h + p_0 \cdot m^h = p \cdot \bar{x}^h + p_0 \cdot \bar{m}^h, \quad h = 1, \ldots, n, \quad \text{and}$$

$$\left. \sum_{h=1}^{n} x^h = \sum_{h=1}^{n} \bar{x}^h , \qquad \sum_{h=1}^{n} m^h = \sum_{h=1}^{n} \bar{m}^h \right\}$$

We note that the condition $D_2 v^h(x^h, m^h, \pi; \gamma^h, u^h) = |D_a v^h(x^h, m^h, \pi; \gamma^h, u^h)| \cdot p_0$ can be obtained from $D_1 v^h(x^h, m^h, \pi; \gamma^h, u^h) = |D_a v^h(x^h, m^h, \pi; \gamma^h, u^h)| \cdot p$ and $\Sigma_{j=1}^{\ell} p_j + p_0 = 1$ for each agent h. Furthermore, the admissibility of money $\Sigma_{h=1}^{n} m^h = \Sigma_{h=1}^{n} \bar{m}^h$ follows from

$p \cdot x^h + p_0 \cdot m^h = p \cdot \bar{x}^h + p_0 \cdot \bar{m}^h$, $h = 1, \ldots, n$, $\Sigma_{h=1}^n x^h = \Sigma_{h=1}^n \bar{x}^h$, and $\pi = (p, p_0) \gg 0$. Hence, we rewrite (4) as the following

$$\Phi(E) = \Big\{ (x, m, \pi) \in P^n \times R_+^n \times \Pi : D_1 v^h(x^h, m^h, \pi; \gamma^h, u^h)$$

$$= |D_a v^h(x^h, m^h, \pi; \gamma^h, u^h)| \cdot p,$$

(4')

$$p \cdot x^h + p_0 \cdot m^h = p \cdot \bar{x}^h + p_0 \cdot \bar{m}^h, \quad h = 1, \ldots, n, \quad \text{and}$$

$$\sum_{h=1}^n x^h = \sum_{h=1}^n \bar{x}^h \Big\}$$

For every money economy $E \in \mathscr{E}$, we define a map $\psi_E : P^n \times R_+^n \times \Pi \rightarrow R^{\ell n + n + \ell}$ by

$$\psi_E(x, m, \pi)$$

$$= \Big(D_1 v^h(x^h, m^h, \pi; \gamma^h, u^h) - |D_a v^h(x^h, m^h, \pi; \gamma^h, u^h)| \cdot p,$$

(5)

$$p \cdot x^h + p_0 \cdot m^h - p \cdot \bar{x}^h - p_0 \cdot \bar{m}^h, \quad h = 1, \ldots, n,$$

$$\sum_{h=1}^n x^h - \sum_{h=1}^n \bar{x}^h \Big)$$

Obviously, $\psi_E \in C^1(P^n \times R_+^n \times \Pi, R^{\ell n + n + \ell})$. From (4') and (5), we have $\Phi(E) = \psi_E^{-1}(0)$ for every money economy $E \in \mathscr{E}$.

PROPOSITION 5. The map $\psi_E: P^n \times R^n_+ \times \Pi \to R^{\ell n+n+\ell}$ defined by (5) is proper[9] for every $E \in \mathscr{E}$. In particular, $\Phi(E)$ is a compact subset in $P^n \times R^n_+ \times \Pi$ for every $E \in \mathscr{E}$.

Proof. Let $K \subset R^{\ell n+n+\ell}$ be a compact set, then $\psi_E^{-1}(K) = \{(x,m,\pi) \in P^n \times R^n_+ \times \Pi$: $D_1 v^h(x^h, m^h, \pi; \gamma^h, u^h) = \alpha^h + |D_a v^h(x^h, m^h, \pi; \gamma^h, u^h)| \cdot p$, $p \cdot x^h + p_0 \cdot m^h = \beta^h + p \cdot \bar{x}^h + p_0 \cdot \bar{m}^h$, $h = 1, \ldots, n$, $\Sigma_{h=1}^n x^h = \delta + \Sigma_{h=1}^n \bar{x}^h$ for every $k = (\alpha, \beta, \delta) \in K$, where $\alpha = (\alpha^1, \ldots, \alpha^n) \in R^{\ell n}$, $\beta = (\beta^1, \ldots, \beta^n) \in R^n$ and $\delta = (\delta_1, \ldots, \delta_\ell) \in R^\ell\}$ for any $E \in \mathscr{E}$. If $\psi_E^{-1}(K) = \phi$, it is trivial. Suppose $\psi_E^{-1}(K) \neq \phi$, then $\psi_E^{-1}(K) = \psi_E^{-1}(K^*)$ since $\psi_E^{-1}(k) = \phi$ if $k \notin K^*$, where $K^* = \{k = (\alpha, \beta, \delta) \in K$: $\alpha^h < 0$, $\alpha^h + |D_a v^h(x^h, m^h, \pi; \gamma^h, u^h)| \cdot p \gg 0$, $\beta^h + p \cdot \bar{x}^h + p_0 \cdot \bar{m}^h > 0$, $h = 1, \ldots, n$, and $\delta + \Sigma_{h=1}^n \bar{x}^h \gg 0\}$. Furthermore, $\psi_E^{-1}(K)$ is closed in $P^n \times R^n_+ \times \Pi$ since ψ_E is class C^1. That is, there is a sequence $\{(x^q, m^q, \pi^q)\}$ with $(x^q, m^q, \pi^q) \in \psi_E^{-1}(K)$ for every q such that (x^q, m^q, π^q) converges to $(x^o, m^o, \pi^o) \in \psi_E^{-1}(K)$. It is clear that x^o will not take values on the boundary of the closure of P^n by A.2(i). Now, we claim $\pi^o \gg 0$. From A.1, $\mathscr{M}(\Pi \times P)$ is tight (see [5]). That is, there exists an element $\gamma^{ho} \in \mathscr{M}(\Pi \times P)$ such that $\gamma^h(\pi^q)$ converges weakly to γ^{ho}. Without loss of generality, we let $\gamma^{ho} = \gamma^h(\pi^o)$. Consider

[9] A continuous mapping f from a topological space X to a topological space Y is called proper if the inverse image of every compact set is compact.

the expected utility function of the action (x^{ho}, m^{ho}) at π^o,

$$v^h(x^{ho}, m^{ho}, \pi^o; \gamma^h, u^h) = \int_{\Pi \times P} \hat{u}^h(x^{ho}, m^{ho}; \cdot, \cdot)\, d\gamma^h(\pi^o; \cdot, \cdot)$$

which is well defined and class C^{k-1} with $k > 2$ in (x^{ho}, m^{ho}). By Propositions 2 and 3, $D_a v^h(x^{ho}, m^{ho}, \pi^o; \gamma^h, u^h) \gg 0$. Since $(x^o, m^o, \pi^o) \in \psi_E^{-1}(K)$, we have

$$D_1 v^h(x^{ho}, m^{ho}, \pi^o; \gamma^h, u^h) = \alpha^h + |D_a v^h(x^{ho}, m^{ho}, \pi^o; \gamma^h, u^h)| \cdot p^o$$

for each h. This proves $\pi^o \gg 0$. Furthermore, $\psi_E^{-1}(K)$ is bounded by definition. Therefore, $\psi_E^{-1}(K)$ is compact in $P^n \times R_+^n \times \Pi$ for every $E \in \mathscr{E}$. In particular, let $K = \{0\}$, $\Phi(E) = \psi_E^{-1}(0)$ is compact in $P^n \times R_+^n \times \Pi$ for every $E \in \mathscr{E}$.

Q. E. D.

Chapter IV

MAIN THEOREMS

In this chapter we study the structure of the set of temporary monetary equilibria. It is well known that not every equilibrium of an economy varies locally in a continuous and unique manner with the parameters which define the economy. For example, looking into the Edgeworth box for two agents and two commodities, it is easy to construct an economy with a continuum of equilibria. So, a natural question arises. How "large" is the subspace of economies which satisfies the above determinate equilibrium properties? For the general equilibrium model, this was answered by Debreu in [9]. That is, the complement of the space of Arrow-Debreu economies which satisfy the above determinate equilibrium properties is a "negligible" set which, in finite dimensional framework, means a closed set of Lebesgue measure zero. We claim an analogous conclusion for the (infinite dimensional) space of money economies in the temporary equilibrium framework. In particular, we prove local uniqueness and stability of extended temporary monetary equilibrium for "almost all" economies in $\mathscr{E}$, as well as the existence theorem for every economy in $\mathscr{E}$. The concept of "almost all" is defined precisely by a regularity condition on the map ψ_E below. As corollaries we also obtain local uniqueness, stability and existence of (classical) temporary monetary equilibrium. The techniques we use are similar to Smale's [53] in which, however, the utility functions are independent of money and price parameters. For local uniqueness, there is no need to assume concavity on the direct utility function nor any restrictive assumption such as gross substitutability among commodities (see [2], for instance). The stability or continuity property follows from an application of the implicit function theorem.

IV(a) Genericity of Regular Money Economies

We first recall a concept of transversality in differential topology. Let Z be a submanifold (see [1] for a definition) of Y, $f \in C^1(X,Y)$ is said to be transversal to Z at $x \in X$, denoted by $f \pitchfork_x Z$, if either $y = f(x) \notin Z$, or $y = f(x) \in Z$ and $Df(x)[T_x X] + T_y Z = T_y Y$ where $T_x X$ and $T_y Y$ denote the tangent spaces of X at x and Y at y, respectively. If $f \pitchfork_x Z$ for every $x \in X$, $f \pitchfork Z$. Actually, we apply the concept of transversality only in the very special sense of the above. That is, Z is just a single point $\{y\}$, and therefore its tangent space is the zero subspace of $T_y Y$. Thus, f is transversal to y if $Df(x)[T_x X] = T_y Y$ for all $x \in f^{-1}(y)$, which is to say that y is a regular value of f. So transversality includes the notion of regularity as a special case. In fact, f is regular if and only if $f \pitchfork y$ for every $y \in Y$. In view of the space of economies $\mathscr{E}$, we have a family of C^1 maps $\psi_E : P^n \times R^n_+ \times \Pi \to R^{\ell n+n+\ell}$ defined by (5). In other words, ψ_E is parameterized by the space $\mathscr{E}$. We need a few more definitions. An element $E \in \mathscr{E}$ is called a regular money economy if and only if the associated map ψ_E defined by (5) is transversal to the origin, i.e., $\psi_E \pitchfork 0$. Moreover, the space of regular money economies is denoted by the set $\mathscr{R} = \{E \in \mathscr{E} : \psi_E \pitchfork 0\}$ and the space of classical regular money economies is $\mathscr{R}_0 = \mathscr{R} \cap \mathscr{E}_0$. By a theorem of differential topology (for instance, see [1], p. 45), $\psi_E^{-1}(0) = \Phi(E)$ is a C^1 "submanifold" of the space $P^n \times R^n_+ \times \Pi$ for every $E \in \mathscr{R}$. We claim that the subspace of money economies satisfying a transversality requirement (i.e., the space of regular money economies $\mathscr{R}$) is open and dense in the "strong" topology defined on the space of economies. Indeed, $\mathscr{R}$ is quite a large subset of the space of all money economies $\mathscr{E}$ and also, the complement of $\mathscr{R}$ in $\mathscr{E}$ is a closed set with empty interior. The latter is exactly the notion of a "negligible" set from a topological viewpoint. We like to note that the measure theoretic concept of a negligible set or a closed set of Lebesgue measure zero used by Debreu and others is not available for infinite dimensional spaces. Hence, the best we can show at this point is that the set of regular money economies $\mathscr{R}$ is open and dense in the space of all money economies $\mathscr{E}$. In other words, every money economy can be approximated by a regular money economy and every regular money economy is still regular under small perturbation of the economic characteristics of the model. To prove the density and openness of $\mathscr{R}$ in $\mathscr{E}$, we shall use some notions and properties of inverse limit and restriction operation. The idea is that the space of economies $\mathscr{E}$ can be characterized as the inverse limit space of a sequence of more concrete spaces of auxiliary economies $\mathscr{E}_\alpha$ which is defined by an operation of compact restriction of function spaces. Many important features of the space of economies then can be induced from those in the spaces of auxiliary economies by a limiting process.

First, we give some basic definitions. Let X_α be a topological space and f_α be a continuous map from X_α into $X_{\alpha-1}$ for each index α. The sequence $\{X_\alpha, f_\alpha\}$ is called an <u>inverse limit sequence</u>. The <u>inverse limit space</u> of the sequence $\{X_\alpha, f_\alpha\}$ is a subset of the product $\Pi_\alpha X_\alpha$, denoted $\lim_{\leftarrow} X_\alpha$, such that $f_\alpha(x_\alpha) = x_{\alpha-1}$ for each α and $x_\alpha \in X_\alpha$, $x_{\alpha-1} \in X_{\alpha-1}$. If X_α are Hausdorff, then $\lim_{\leftarrow} X_\alpha$ is a closed subset of the product $\Pi_\alpha X_\alpha$ (see [60], pp. 217-219). Let $\{X_\alpha, f_\alpha\}$ and $\{Y_\alpha, g_\alpha\}$ be inverse limit sequences, and $\{\xi_\alpha\}$ be a sequence of mappings such that $\xi_\alpha : X_\alpha \to Y_\alpha$ and the following diagram

$$\begin{array}{ccccccc}
\cdots \leftarrow & X_{\alpha-1} & \xleftarrow{\quad f_\alpha \quad} & X_\alpha & \leftarrow \cdots \\
 & \Big\downarrow \xi_{\alpha-1} & & \Big\downarrow \xi_\alpha & \\
\cdots \leftarrow & Y_{\alpha-1} & \xleftarrow{\quad g_\alpha \quad} & Y_\alpha & \leftarrow \cdots
\end{array}$$

is commutative, that is, $\xi_{\alpha-1} \circ f_\alpha = g_\alpha \circ \xi_\alpha$ for each α. Then the induced mapping, denoted

$$\lim_{\leftarrow} \xi_\alpha : \lim_{\leftarrow} X_\alpha \to \lim_{\leftarrow} Y_\alpha ,$$

is given by

$$\lim_{\leftarrow} \xi_\alpha((x_\alpha)) = (\xi_\alpha(x_\alpha)) .$$

We know $(\xi_\alpha(x_\alpha)) \in \lim_{\leftarrow} Y_\alpha$ if $(x_\alpha) \in \lim_{\leftarrow} X_\alpha$, by virtue of the requirement $\xi_{\alpha-1} \circ f_\alpha = g_\alpha \circ \xi_\alpha$ for each α. It is clear that if each ξ_α is continuous, so is $\lim_{\leftarrow} \xi_\alpha$.

Let $u \in C^1(R^m, R^n)$. Since R^m is locally compact, we write $\{K_\alpha\}$ as a sequence of compact subsets in R^m with $K_{\alpha-1} \subset K_\alpha$ for each α and $R^m = \cup_\alpha K_\alpha$. Denote $u_\alpha = u | K_\alpha \in \tilde{C}^1(K_\alpha, R^n)$ for each α where $\tilde{C}^1(K_\alpha, R^n)$ is a family of continuously differentiable functions from K_α to R^n with the following closeness property: Given $u_\alpha, u'_\alpha \in \tilde{C}^1(K_\alpha, R^n)$, if u_α is close to u'_α, then there exists a positive continuous real-valued function $\epsilon_\alpha : K_\alpha - \text{int } K_{\alpha-1} \to R$ such that $\| D^k u_\alpha(x) - D^k u'_\alpha(x) \| < \epsilon_\alpha(x)$ for all $x \in K_\alpha - \text{int } K_{\alpha-1}$ and $k = 0, 1$. Let $f_\alpha : \tilde{C}^1(K_\alpha, R^n) \to \tilde{C}^1(K_{\alpha-1}, R^n)$ be an operation of restriction such that $f_\alpha(u_\alpha) = u_{\alpha-1} = u_\alpha | K_{\alpha-1}$. It will be shown that $\{\tilde{C}^1(K_\alpha, R^n), f_\alpha\}$ is an inverse limit sequence and $C^1(R^m, R^n)$ is (topologically) equivalent[10] to the inverse limit space $\lim_{\leftarrow} \tilde{C}^1(K_\alpha, R^n)$. The former statement follows from the continuity of f_α for each α, and the latter requires that $C^1(R^m, R^n)$ with the C^1 compact-open topology (resp. Whitney C^1 topology) is homeomorphic to $\lim_{\leftarrow} \tilde{C}^1(K_\alpha, R^n)$ with the relative C^1 product topology (resp. C^1 box topology).[11] In summary, we have the following two lemmas:

LEMMA 1. $\{\tilde{C}^1(K_\alpha, R^n), f_\alpha\}$ <u>is an inverse limit sequence of the spaces</u> $\tilde{C}^1(K_\alpha, R^n)$ for each α.

---

[10] As we know, a homeomorphism f from X to Y provides simultaneously a one-to-one and onto map for the underlying spaces and the topologies. Hence every property of X expressed entirely in terms of set operations and open sets (that is, any topological property of X) is also possessed by each space homeomorphic to X. Two topological spaces are (topologically) equivalent if and only if they are homeomorphic.

[11] For definitions of product topology and box topology on a product space, see [40].

Proof. It is sufficient to show that the map $f_\alpha : \tilde{C}^1(K_\alpha, R^n) \to \tilde{C}^1(K_{\alpha-1}, R^n)$ given by $f_\alpha(u_\alpha) = u_{\alpha-1} = u_\alpha | K_{\alpha-1}$ is continuous. We have to prove that, if $N_{\alpha-1} \subset \tilde{C}^1(K_{\alpha-1}, R^n)$ is open, then $f_\alpha^{-1}(N_{\alpha-1})$ is open in $\tilde{C}^1(K_\alpha, R^n)$. Clearly, we may assume that $N_{\alpha-1}$ is of the form

$$N_{\alpha-1} = N(u_{\alpha-1}, \epsilon_{\alpha-1})$$

$$= \{u'_{\alpha-1} \in \tilde{C}^1(K_{\alpha-1}, R^n): \|D^k u_{\alpha-1}(x) - D^k u'_{\alpha-1}(x)\| < \epsilon_{\alpha-1}(x)$$

$$\text{for all } x \in K_{\alpha-1} - \text{int } K_{\alpha-2}, \ k = 0, 1\} ,$$

where $u_{\alpha-1} \in \tilde{C}^1(K_{\alpha-1}, R^n)$, $\epsilon: R^m \to R$ is a positive continuous function and $\epsilon_{\alpha-1} = \epsilon | K_{\alpha-1} - \text{int } K_{\alpha-2}$, and $\| \cdot \|$ is the norm on $C^1(R^m, R^n)$. Therefore,

$$f_\alpha^{-1}(N_{\alpha-1}) = \{u'_\alpha \in \tilde{C}^1(K_\alpha, R^n): \|D^k f_\alpha(u_\alpha)(x) - D^k f_\alpha(u'_\alpha)(x)\| < \epsilon_{\alpha-1}(x)$$

$$\text{for all } x \in K_{\alpha-1} - \text{int } K_{\alpha-2}, \ k = 0, 1\} .$$

It is obvious that $f_\alpha^{-1}(N_{\alpha-1})$ is open in $\tilde{C}^1(K_\alpha, R^n)$. Q.E.D.

LEMMA 2. $C^1(R^m, R^n)$ <u>with the</u> C^1 <u>compact-open topology (resp. Whitney</u> C^1 <u>topology) is (topologically) equivalent to</u> $\lim_{\leftarrow} \tilde{C}^1(K_\alpha, R^n)$ <u>with the relative</u> C^1 <u>product topology (resp. relative</u> C^1 <u>box topology).</u>

Proof. Let N_β be an open neighborhood in $\tilde{C}^1(K_\beta, R^n)$ as defined in the proof of Lemma 1. Then the sets of the following type

$$\mathrm{Proj}_\beta^{-1}(N_\beta) \cap \lim_{\leftarrow} \tilde{C}^1(K_\alpha, R^n)$$

$$= \{(u_\alpha) \in \lim_{\leftarrow} \tilde{C}^1(K_\alpha, R^n) : \|D^k u_\beta(x) - D^k u'_\beta(x)\| < \epsilon_\beta(x)$$

$$\text{for all } x \in K_\beta - \mathrm{int}\, K_{\beta-1},\ k = 0, 1\} ,$$

form a subbase for the relative C^1 product topology on $\lim_{\leftarrow} \tilde{C}^1(K_\alpha, R^n)$, where Proj_β is the projection map of a space along its β-th coordinate. Similarly, the sets of the following type

$$\prod_\alpha N_\alpha \cap \lim_{\leftarrow} \tilde{C}^1(K_\alpha, R^n)$$

$$= \{(u_\alpha) \in \lim_{\leftarrow} \tilde{C}^1(K_\alpha, R^n) : \|D^k u_\alpha(x) - D^k u'_\alpha(x)\| < \epsilon_\alpha(x)$$

$$\text{for all } \alpha \text{ and } x \in K_\alpha - \mathrm{int}\, K_{\alpha-1},\ k = 0, 1\}$$

generate a base for the relative C^1 box topology on

$$\lim_{\leftarrow} \tilde{C}^1(K_\alpha, R^n)$$

Let h be a map from the function space $C^1(R^m, R^n)$ with the C^1 compact-open topology (resp. Whitney C^1 topology) to the space $\lim_{\leftarrow} \tilde{C}^1(K_\alpha, R^n)$ with the relative C^1 product topology (resp. relative C^1 box topology) such that $h(u) = (u_\alpha) = (u| K_\alpha)$. We claim that h is a homeomorphism. It is clear that h is one-to-one onto, and h^{-1} is continuous. Taking open sets of the form $V = \mathrm{Proj}_\beta^{-1}(N_\beta) \cap \lim_{\leftarrow} \tilde{C}^1(K_\alpha, R^n)$ in $\lim_{\leftarrow} \tilde{C}^1(K_\alpha, R^n)$, we have

$$h^{-1}(V) = \{u \in C^1(R^m, R^n): \|D^k u(x) - D^k u'(x)\| < \epsilon(x) \quad \text{for all}$$

$$x \in K_\beta - \mathrm{int}\, K_{\beta-1}, \quad k = 0, 1\} ,$$

which is open in the C^1 compact-open topology. If, instead, we take the open sets of the form $V = \Pi_\alpha N_\alpha \cap \lim_{\leftarrow} \tilde{C}^1(K_\alpha, R^n)$, then

$$h^{-1}(V) = \{u \in C^1(R^m, R^n): \|D^k u(x) - D^k u'(x)\| < \epsilon(x)$$

$$\text{for all} \quad x \in R^m, \quad k = 0, 1\}$$

which is open in the Whitney C^1 topology. Hence h is continuous. Q.E.D.

In the following proposition, we shall use Lemma 1 and Lemma 2 to prove that "almost all" money economies are regular. For convenience we use the same notation for the space of money economies and the inverse limit of the spaces of auxiliary money economies since they are (topologically) equivalent.

PROPOSITION 6. $\mathscr{R}$ <u>is open and dense in</u> $\mathscr{E}$ <u>with respect to the "strong" topology (defined in</u> III(b)).

<u>Proof.</u> Since P and Π are locally compact, we let $\{K_\alpha\}$ and $\{L_\alpha\}$ be the sequences of compact subsets in P and Π, respectively, such that $K_\alpha \subset K_{\alpha+1}$, $L_\alpha \subset L_{\alpha-1}$ and $P = \cup_\alpha K_\alpha$, $\Pi = \cup_\alpha L_\alpha$. For each $u^h \in C^k(P \times P, R)$ with $k > 2$, let $u_\alpha^h = u^h | K_\alpha \times K_\alpha \in \tilde{C}^k(K_\alpha \times K_\alpha, R)$. Similarly, for each $\gamma^h \in C^1(\Pi, \mathscr{M}(\Pi \times P))$, let $\gamma_\alpha^h = \gamma^h | L_\alpha \in \tilde{C}^1(L_\alpha, \mathscr{M}(\Pi \times P))$. The spaces $\tilde{C}^k(K_\alpha \times K_\alpha, R)$ and $\tilde{C}^1(L_\alpha, \mathscr{M}(\Pi \times P))$ are metrizable and separable, hence they are second countable (see [40]). Moreover, the spaces $C^k(P \times P, R)$ and $C^1(\Pi, \mathscr{M}(\Pi \times P))$ with the C^k and C^1 compact-open topologies are (topologically) equivalent to the inverse limits of the sequences $\{\tilde{C}^k(K_\alpha \times K_\alpha, R), f_\alpha\}$ and $\{\tilde{C}^1(L_\alpha, \mathscr{M}(\Pi \times P)), g_\alpha\}$, respectively. That is, $f_\alpha: \tilde{C}^k(K_\alpha \times K_\alpha, R) \to \tilde{C}^k(K_{\alpha-1} \times K_{\alpha-1}, R)$ and $g_\alpha: \tilde{C}^1(L_\alpha, \mathscr{M}(\Pi \times P)) \to \tilde{C}^1(L_{\alpha-1}, \mathscr{M}(\Pi \times P))$ defined by $f_\alpha(u_\alpha^h) = u_{\alpha-1}^h = u_\alpha^h | K_{\alpha-1} \times K_{\alpha-1}$ and $g_\alpha(\gamma_\alpha^h) = \gamma_{\alpha-1}^h = \gamma_\alpha^h | L_{\alpha-1}$ are continuous (see Lemma 1), and the topologies of $C^k(P \times P, R)$ and $C^1(\Pi, \mathscr{M}(\Pi \times P))$ induced by the product topologies of

$\Pi_\alpha \tilde{C}^k(K_\alpha \times K_\alpha, R)$ and $\Pi_\alpha \tilde{C}^1(L_\alpha, \mathcal{M}(\Pi \times P))$ are equivalent to the C^k and C^1 compact-open topologies, respectively (see Lemma 2). Define

$$\mathcal{U}_\alpha = \left\{ u^h_\alpha \in \tilde{C}^k(K_\alpha \times K_\alpha, R) : u^h_\alpha = u^h | K_\alpha \times K_\alpha \text{ and } u^h \in \mathcal{U} \right\}$$

and

$$\Gamma_\alpha = \left\{ \gamma^h_\alpha \in \tilde{C}^1(L_\alpha, \mathcal{M}(\Pi \times P)) : \gamma^h_\alpha = \gamma^h | L_\alpha \text{ and } \gamma^h \in \Gamma \right\} .$$

Clearly, $\mathcal{U}$ and Γ are the inverse limit of $\{\mathcal{U}_\alpha, f'_\alpha\}$ and $\{\Gamma_\alpha, g'_\alpha\}$, respectively, where $f'_\alpha = f_\alpha | \mathcal{U}_\alpha$ and $g'_\alpha = g_\alpha | \Gamma_\alpha$. Moreover, let $R_+ = \cup_\alpha M_\alpha$ with M_α compact and $M_\alpha \subset M_{\alpha+1}$, where M_α is constructed in a way such that the corresponding future plan is feasible. That is, given an action in $K_\alpha \times M_\alpha$ and a future event in $\Pi \times P$, the corresponding future plan of every agent is in the compact set K_α, which is computed from the first order condition of utility maximization subject to the budget constraint for the future period (compare with the expression (1) in II(c)). For each $u^h_\alpha \in \mathcal{U}_\alpha$ and $\gamma^h_\alpha \in \Gamma_\alpha$, if $\pi \in L_\alpha$ is the current price system, we can define an expected utility function on the compact domain $K_\alpha \times M_\alpha \times L_\alpha$, denoted v^h_α, as follows:

$$v^h_\alpha(x^h, m^h, \pi; \gamma^h_\alpha, u^h_\alpha) = \int_{\Pi \times P} \hat{u}^h_\alpha(x^h, m^h; \cdot, \cdot)\, d\gamma^h_\alpha(\pi; \cdot, \cdot)$$

It is obvious that for each $\gamma^h_\alpha \in \Gamma_\alpha$ and $u^h_\alpha \in \mathcal{U}_\alpha$,

$v_\alpha^h(\cdot,\cdot,\cdot;\gamma_\alpha^h, u_\alpha^h)$ satisfies the properties stated in Propositions 2 and 3 restricted to the compact domain $K_\alpha \times M_\alpha \times L_\alpha$. In addition, we also need to check that v_α^h depends on $(\gamma_\alpha^h, u_\alpha^h)$ in a continuously differentiable fashion. Observe that the evaluation maps of γ_α^h and u_α^h are C^1 and C^k with respect to the induced C^1 and C^k compact-open topologies on Γ_α and $\mathscr{U}_\alpha$, respectively (see [1], p. 25). Hence v_α^h is class C^1.

Let $\mathscr{E}_\alpha = (\Gamma_\alpha \times \mathscr{U}_\alpha \times P \times R_+)^n$, then the space of money economies $\mathscr{E}$ is the inverse limit space of $\{\mathscr{E}_\alpha, F_\alpha\}$ where $F_\alpha : \mathscr{E}_\alpha \to \mathscr{E}_{\alpha-1}$ is defined by

$$F_\alpha = (\underbrace{f'_\alpha, \ldots, f'_\alpha}_{n \text{ times}}, \underbrace{g'_\alpha, \ldots, g'_\alpha}_{n \text{ times}}, \text{id})$$

and id, the identity map, from $P^n \times R_+^n$ to $P^n \times R_+^n$. Define the sequence $\{\mathscr{R}_\alpha, G_\alpha\}$ as $\mathscr{R}_\alpha = \{E_\alpha \in \mathscr{E}_\alpha : \psi_{E_\alpha} \pitchfork 0\}$, $G_\alpha = F_\alpha | \mathscr{R}_\alpha$ and $\psi_{E_\alpha} = \psi_E | K_\alpha^n \times M_\alpha^n \times L_\alpha$. Then $\mathscr{R}$ is the inverse limit of $\{\mathscr{R}_\alpha, G_\alpha\}$. We claim that $\mathscr{R}_\alpha$ is open and dense in $\mathscr{E}_\alpha$ for each α. We apply the transversality density theorem, 19.1 of [1], p. 48. Conditions (1), (2), and (3) of Theorem 19.1 are satisfied. We need to check condition (4) of Theorem 19.1. First, let $\psi_\alpha : \mathscr{E}_\alpha \times K_\alpha^n \times M_\alpha^n \times L_\alpha \to R^{\ell n+n+\ell}$ defined by $\psi_\alpha(E_\alpha, x, m, \pi) = \psi_{E_\alpha}(x, m, \pi)$ for each $E_\alpha \in \mathscr{E}_\alpha$

and $(x, m, \pi) \in K_\alpha^n \times M_\alpha^n \times L_\alpha$ be the evaluation map of ψ_{E_α}. It is clear that ψ_α is class C^1 since v_α^h is class C^1 for each h, and ψ_{E_α} has compact domain for every $E_\alpha \in \mathscr{E}_\alpha$ (for instance, see [1], p. 25). Notice that ψ_α has C^1 extension on the boundary of $\mathscr{E}_\alpha \times K_\alpha^n \times M_\alpha^n \times L_\alpha$ by the construction of the space $\mathscr{E}_\alpha$ from $\mathscr{E}$. We go on to prove that the evaluation map ψ_α is transversal to 0, i.e., $\psi_{E_\alpha} \pitchfork 0$. By definition, ψ_α is given by

$$\psi_\alpha^h(E_\alpha, x, m, \pi) = \Big(D_1 v_\alpha^h(x^h, m^h, \pi; \gamma^h, u^h) - |D_a v_\alpha^h(x^h, m^h, \pi; \gamma^h, u^h)| \cdot p$$

$$p \cdot x^h + p_0 \cdot m^h - p \cdot \bar{x}^h - p_0 \cdot \bar{m}^h, \quad h = 1, \ldots, n,$$

$$\sum_{h=1}^{n} x^h - \sum_{h=1}^{n} \bar{x}^h \Big)$$

Its derivative at (E_α, x, m, π), i.e.,

$$D\psi_\alpha(E_\alpha, x, m, \pi): T_{(E_\alpha, x, m, \pi)}(\mathscr{E}_\alpha \times K_\alpha^n \times M_\alpha^n \times L_\alpha) \to R^{\ell n + n + \ell}$$

is defined by

$$D\psi_\alpha(E_\alpha, x, m, \pi)(\dot{E}_\alpha, \dot{x}, \dot{m}, \dot{\pi})$$

$$= \left(\frac{\partial^2 v_\alpha^h}{\partial x_k^h \partial E_\alpha} \dot{E}_\alpha - \left(\sum_{i=1}^{\ell} \frac{\partial^2 v_\alpha^h}{\partial x_i^h \partial E_\alpha} + \frac{\partial^2 v_\alpha^h}{\partial m^h \partial E_\alpha} \right) p_k \dot{E}_\alpha \right.$$

$$+ \sum_{j=1}^{\ell} \frac{\partial^2 v_\alpha^h}{\partial x_k^h \partial x_j^h} \dot{x}_j^h - \sum_{j=1}^{\ell} \left(\sum_{i=1}^{\ell} \frac{\partial^2 v_\alpha^h}{\partial x_i^h \partial x_j^h} + \frac{\partial^2 v_\alpha^h}{\partial m^h \partial x_j^h} \right) p_k \dot{x}_j$$

$$+ \frac{\partial^2 v_\alpha^h}{\partial x_k^h \partial m^h} \dot{m}^h - \left(\sum_{i=1}^{\ell} \frac{\partial^2 v_\alpha^h}{\partial x_i^h \partial m^h} + \frac{\partial^2 v_\alpha^h}{\partial m^h \partial m^h} \right) p_k \dot{m}^h$$

$$+ \sum_{j=0}^{\ell} \frac{\partial^2 v_\alpha^h}{\partial x_k^h \partial p_j} \dot{p}_j - \sum_{j=0}^{\ell} \left(\sum_{i=1}^{\ell} \frac{\partial^2 v_\alpha^h}{\partial x_i^h \partial p_j} + \frac{\partial^2 v_\alpha^h}{\partial m^h \partial p_j} \right) p_k \dot{p}_j$$

$$- \left(\sum_{i=1}^{\ell} \frac{\partial v_\alpha^h}{\partial x_i^h} + \frac{\partial v_\alpha^h}{\partial m^h} \right) \dot{p}_k , \quad k = 1, \ldots, \ell , \quad h = 1, \ldots, n ,$$

$$\dot{p}(\bar{x}^h - x^h) + p(\dot{\bar{x}}^h - \dot{x}^h) + \dot{p}_0(\bar{m}^h - m^h) + p_0(\dot{\bar{m}}^h - \dot{m}^h) , \quad h = 1, \ldots, n ,$$

$$\left. \sum_{h=1}^{n} \dot{\bar{x}}^h - \sum_{h=1}^{n} \dot{x}^h \right) ,$$

where $(\dot{E}_\alpha, \dot{x}, \dot{m}, \dot{\pi}) \in T_{(E_\alpha, x, m, \pi)} (\mathscr{E}_\alpha \times K_\alpha^n \times M_\alpha^n \times L_\alpha)$ and $\dot{E}_\alpha = (\dot{\gamma}_\alpha, \dot{u}_\alpha, \dot{\bar{x}}, \dot{\bar{m}})$. Without loss of generality, we take $\dot{E}_\alpha = (0, 0, \dot{\bar{x}}, \dot{\bar{m}})$ and $\dot{x} = 0$, $\dot{m} = 0$. Then

$$D\psi_\alpha(E_\alpha, x, m, \pi)(\dot{E}_\alpha, \dot{x}, \dot{m}, \dot{\pi}) = D\psi_\alpha(E_\alpha, x, m, \pi)((0, 0, \dot{\bar{x}}, \dot{\bar{m}}), 0, 0, \dot{\pi})$$

$$= \left(\sum_{j=0}^{\ell} \frac{\partial^2 v_\alpha^h}{\partial x_k^h \partial p_j} \dot{p}_j - \sum_{j=0}^{\ell} \left(\sum_{i=1}^{\ell} \frac{\partial^2 v_\alpha^h}{\partial x_i^h \partial p_j} + \frac{\partial^2 v_\alpha^h}{\partial m^h \partial p_j} \right) p_k \dot{p}_j \right.$$

$$- \left(\sum_{i=1}^{\ell} \frac{\partial v_\alpha^h}{\partial x_i^h} + \frac{\partial v_\alpha^h}{\partial m^h} \right) \dot{p}_k , \quad k = 1, \ldots, \ell , \quad h = 1, \ldots, n ,$$

$$\dot{p}\cdot(\bar{x}^h - x^h) + p\cdot\dot{\bar{x}}^h + \dot{p}_0\cdot(\bar{m}^h - m^h) + p_0\cdot\dot{\bar{m}}^h, \quad h = 1,\ldots,n, \quad \sum_{h=1}^{n}\dot{\bar{x}}^h \Big)$$

For each $(a,b,c) \in R^{\ell n+n+\ell}$ with $a = (a^1,\ldots,a^n) \in R^{\ell n}$, $b = (b^1,\ldots,b^n) \in R^n$ and $c = (c_1,\ldots,c_\ell) \in R^\ell$, there exists $((0,0,\dot{\bar{x}},\dot{\bar{m}}),0,0,\dot{\pi}) \in T_{(E_\alpha,x,m,\pi)}(\mathscr{E}_\alpha \times K_\alpha^n \times M_\alpha^n \times L_\alpha)$ such that

$$D\psi_\alpha(E_\alpha,x,m,\pi)((0,0,\dot{\bar{x}},\dot{\bar{m}}),0,0,\dot{\pi}) = (a,b,c),$$

since

$$\sum_{i=1}^{\ell}\frac{\partial v^h}{\partial x_i^h} + \frac{\partial v^h}{\partial m^h} > 0$$

for each h and $\pi \neq 0$. Therefore, $D\psi_\alpha(E_\alpha,x,m,\pi)$ is surjective on $R^{\ell n+n+\ell}$. In particular, $\psi_\alpha \pitchfork 0$. This shows that condition (4) of the transversal density theorem, 19.1 of [1], is satisfied. Hence $\mathscr{R}_\alpha$ is dense in $\mathscr{E}_\alpha$. The openness of $\mathscr{R}_\alpha$ in $\mathscr{E}_\alpha$ follows from the openness of transversal intersection theorem, 18.2 of [1], p. 47.

Finally, we have to show that the inverse limit of $\{\mathscr{R}_\alpha, G_\alpha\}$ is also open and dense in the inverse limit of $\{\mathscr{E}_\alpha, F_\alpha\}$. From the definitions of $\Gamma_\alpha, \mathscr{U}_\alpha$ and Lemma 2, the spaces Γ and $\mathscr{U}$ with the appropriate Whitney topologies are the inverse limit of the sequences $\{\Gamma_\alpha, g'_\alpha\}$ and $\{\mathscr{U}_\alpha, f'_\alpha\}$ with appropriate box topologies on the product $\Pi_\alpha \Gamma_\alpha$ and $\Pi_\alpha \mathscr{U}_\alpha$, respectively. Therefore, the "strong" topology of $\mathscr{E}$ is induced from the product of the box topology on $\Pi_\alpha(\mathscr{U}_\alpha^n \times \Gamma_\alpha^n)$ and the usual topology on $P^n \times R^n_+$. Let $E \in \mathscr{R}$, then by definition, $E_\alpha \in \mathscr{R}_\alpha$ with $G_\alpha(E_\alpha) = E_{\alpha-1}$ for each α. Since $\mathscr{R}_\alpha$ is open in $\mathscr{E}_\alpha$, there is a neighborhood of E_α in $\mathscr{R}_\alpha$, denoted $N_\alpha(E_\alpha)$, such that $N_\alpha(E_\alpha) \subset \mathscr{R}_\alpha$. Write $N(E) = \Pi_\alpha N_\alpha(E_\alpha) \cap \mathscr{E}$ $= \Pi_\alpha (N_\alpha(u_\alpha) \times N_\alpha(\gamma_\alpha)) \times N((\bar{x}, \bar{m}))$, then $N(E)$ is a neighborhood of E in $\mathscr{E}$ with respect to the "strong" topology. Clearly, $N(E) \subset \Pi_\alpha \mathscr{R}_\alpha \cap \mathscr{E}$. But $\Pi_\alpha \mathscr{R}_\alpha \cap \mathscr{E} = \mathscr{R}$ since $\mathscr{R}_\alpha \subset \mathscr{E}_\alpha$ and $G_\alpha = F_\alpha | \mathscr{R}_\alpha$ for each α (see [60], p. 219). In other words, $\mathscr{R}$ is open in $\mathscr{E}$ in the "strong" topology. Moreover, since $\mathscr{R}_\alpha$ is dense in $\mathscr{E}_\alpha$ for each α, any nonempty open set in $\mathscr{E}_\alpha$ intersects $\mathscr{R}_\alpha$. In other words, for each α there exists $(u'_\alpha, \gamma'_\alpha, \bar{x}', \bar{m}') \in N_\alpha(E_\alpha) \cap \mathscr{R}_\alpha$ for $E_\alpha \in \mathscr{E}_\alpha$. Therefore $(u', \gamma', \bar{x}', \bar{m}') \in \Pi_\alpha N_\alpha(E_\alpha) \cap \mathscr{E} \cap \Pi_\alpha \mathscr{R}_\alpha$ $= N(E) \cap \mathscr{R}$. Hence $\mathscr{R}$ is dense in $\mathscr{E}$ with respect to the "strong" topology. Q.E.D.

IV(b) Local Uniqueness and Stability of Temporary Monetary Equilibrium

We first prove the stability theorem.

THEOREM 1. The extended temporary monetary equilibrium correspondence Φ defined by (4) or (4') is continuous on $\mathscr{R}$, i.e., $\Phi(E)$ is stable for every $E \in \mathscr{R}$ with respect to the "strong" topology.

Proof. For every regular money economy $E \in \mathscr{R}$, we have $\psi_E \pitchfork 0$. By the openness property of $\mathscr{R}$ in $\mathscr{E}$, $\psi_{E'} \pitchfork 0$ for $E' \in \mathscr{R}$ near E. We claim that for E' near E, $\psi_{E'}^{-1}(0)$ and $\psi_E^{-1}(0)$ are close to each other, i.e., the extended temporary monetary equilibrium correspondence restricted to the space of regular money economies is continuous. It has been proven in Proposition 6 that with the "strong" topology defined on $\mathscr{E}$, the evaluation map ψ_α defined by $\psi_\alpha(E_\alpha, x, m, \pi) = \psi_{E_\alpha}(x, m, \pi)$ is class C^1. Moreover, for every $E_\alpha \in \mathscr{R}_\alpha$, ψ_{E_α} is a C^1 local diffeomorphism by the inverse function theorem since

$$D\psi_{E_\alpha}(x, m, \pi)\colon T_{(x,m,\pi)}(K_\alpha^n \times M_\alpha^n \times L_\alpha) \to R^{\ell n + n + \ell}$$

with $(x, m, \pi) \in \psi_{E_\alpha}^{-1}(0)$, is an isomorphism. Hence the stability property of the map $\Phi_\alpha = \Phi \mid \mathscr{R}_\alpha : \mathscr{R}_\alpha \to P^n \times R_+^n \times \Pi$ follows by an application of the implicit function theorem on the evaluation map ψ_α. That is, there exist open sets $N_\alpha \subset \mathscr{R}_\alpha$ and $V \subset K_\alpha^n \times M_\alpha^n \times L_\alpha \subset P^n \times R_+^n \times \Pi$ with $E_\alpha \in N_\alpha$ and $(x, m, \pi) \in K_\alpha^n \times M_\alpha^n \times L_\alpha$, and a C^1 function $\xi_\alpha : N_\alpha \to V$ such that $\psi_\alpha(E'_\alpha, \xi_\alpha(E'_\alpha)) = 0$ for every $E'_\alpha \in N_\alpha$ and $\xi_\alpha(E_\alpha) = (x, m, \pi)$. Since $\Phi_{\alpha-1}(E_{\alpha-1}) \subset \Phi_\alpha(E_\alpha)$ for each α, we have the following diagram

$$\begin{array}{ccc} N_{\alpha-1} & \xleftarrow{\;G_\alpha \mid N_\alpha\;} & N_\alpha \\ \Big\downarrow \xi_{\alpha-1} & & \Big\downarrow \xi_\alpha \\ V & \xleftarrow{\;\text{id}\;} & V \end{array}$$

which is commutative, i.e., $\xi_{\alpha-1} \circ G_\alpha \mid N_\alpha = \text{id} \circ \xi_\alpha$ for each α. This implies that at the inverse limit there is a continuous function $\xi : N \cap \mathscr{R} \to V$ such that $\psi(E', \xi(E')) = 0$ for every $E' \in N \cap \mathscr{R}$ and $\xi(E) = (x, m, \pi)$. Hence the extended equilibrium correspondence Φ is stable for every $E \in \mathscr{R}$ with respect to the "strong" topology. Q. E. D.

COROLLARY 1. The temporary monetary equilibrium correspondence restricted to the space of classical regular money economies is continuous. That is, W(E) defined by (3) is stable for every $E \in \mathscr{R}_0$ with respect to the "strong" topology.

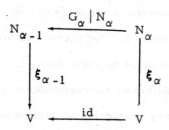

Next, we prove local uniqueness of the extended temporary monetary equilibria for an open and dense subset $\mathscr{R}$ of the space of all money economies $\mathscr{E}$.

THEOREM 2. <u>For every regular money economy</u> $E \in \mathscr{R}$, <u>the extended temporary monetary equilibria are locally unique</u>.

<u>Proof.</u> Since $\Phi(E) = \psi_E^{-1}(0)$ for every $E \in \mathscr{E}$ and $\dim \psi_E^{-1}(0) = \dim (P^n \times R_+^n \times \Pi) - \dim R^{\ell n+n+\ell} = 0$ if 0 is a regular value of the map ψ_E, or equivalently, if $E \in \mathscr{R}$. Thus $\psi_E^{-1}(0)$ is a submanifold with zero dimension for every $E \in \mathscr{R}$. Hence $\Phi(E)$ defined by (4) or (4') is a discrete set. Q.E.D.

COROLLARY 2. <u>For every regular money economy</u> $E \in \mathscr{R}$, <u>the temporary monetary equilibria are locally unique</u>.

<u>Proof.</u> In view of the proof of Corollary 1, $W^*(E) \subset \Phi^*(E) = \psi_E^{*-1}(0)$ for every $E \in \mathscr{E}$. By Theorem 2, $\psi_E^{-1}(0)$ is a discrete set, and hence so is $\psi_E^{*-1}(0)$ for every $E \in \mathscr{R}$. This shows that the set $W^*(E)$ is discrete, and so is $W(E)$, for every $E \in \mathscr{R}$. Q.E.D.

<u>Remark</u> 1. As in [53] and [55], the local uniqueness and stability of equilibria can be obtained under weaker conditions. In particular, there is no need to assume boundary condition A.2(i). Then Theorem 2 is still valid. In our model, since the extended monetary equilibrium correspondence is compact-valued

for every $E \in \mathscr{E}$ (Proposition 5), the finiteness of equilibria follows from the local uniqueness. This, in fact, is a fairly strong conclusion which comes from a boundary condition imposed on the consumption space for every agent in the economy.

IV(c) Existence of Temporary Monetary Equilibrium

Although the extended (or classical) temporary monetary equilibria are locally unique for each regular money economy E, it is possible that $\Phi(E)$ or $W(E)$ is an empty set. This would be a case of no economic interest. It is known [23], [61] that there exists monetary equilibrium for the economies with continuous, concave, monotone direct utility functions and with a compactness requirement on the expectations. In other words, $W(E) \neq \phi$ for every $E \in \mathscr{E}_0$. In this section, we provide a different proof of $W(E) \neq \phi$ for every $E \in \mathscr{E}_0$ in the differentiable framework. The basic idea for proving existence of a temporary monetary equilibrium is in the spirit of counting equations and unknowns. First we construct a specific regular money economy with concave separable utility functions, which has a unique equilibrium and hence the map ψ_E has "degree" one. Next, since any two money economies in the space $\mathscr{E}$ can be connected by a continuous path with respect to the "weak" topology defined on $\mathscr{E}$, one can perform continuous deformations among money economies including the special case with unique equilibrium. This shows that every money economy has the same degree one and hence every money economy has at least one temporary monetary equilibrium. We first prove the following.

PROPOSITION 7. <u>There exists a classical regular money economy with unique temporary monetary equilibrium.</u>

<u>Proof.</u> We prove this proposition by considering a nonempty subset of $\mathcal{U}_0$ for each agent, which contains interperiod additive separable utility functions, denoted by $\mathcal{U}_{00} \subset \mathcal{U}_0 \subset \mathcal{U}$. Define $\mathcal{E}_{00} = (\Gamma \times \mathcal{U}_{00} \times P \times R_+)^n$, then $\mathcal{E}_{00} \subset \mathcal{E}_0 \subset \mathcal{E}$. For an $E = (\gamma, u, \bar{x}, \bar{m}) \in \mathcal{E}_{00}$, let $(\bar{x}, \bar{m})$ be an equilibrium allocation (this is possible if we choose $E = (\gamma, u, \bar{x}, \bar{m})$ with $\gamma^1 = \cdots = \gamma^n$, $u^1 = \cdots = u^n$, $\bar{x}^1 = \cdots = \bar{x}^n$, $\bar{m}^1 = \cdots = \bar{m}^n$). Then there exists a unique $\pi^* \in \Pi$ such that $\psi_E(\bar{x}, \bar{m}, \pi^*) = 0$ since $\gamma^h \in \Gamma$ and $u^h \in \mathcal{U}_0$ for every h. In particular,

$$D_1 v^h(\bar{x}^h, \bar{m}^h, \pi^*; \gamma^h, u^h) = |D_a v^h(\bar{x}^h, \bar{m}^h, \pi^*; \gamma^h, u^h)| \cdot p^*$$

for every agent h. Since $u^h \in \mathcal{U}_{00}$, v^h is differentiably concave by Proposition 4 and additively separable with respect to x^h and (m^h, π). By a well known result of consumer theory on convex preferences or concave utilities (for instance, see [49]), $p^* \cdot x^h + p_0^* \cdot m^h > p^* \cdot \bar{x}^h + p_0^* \cdot \bar{m}^h$ for every h with $(\bar{x}^h, \bar{m}^h) \neq (x^h, m^h)$ and $\psi_E(x, m, \pi^*) = 0$. This is self contradictory. Hence, $(\bar{x}, \bar{m}, \pi^*)$ is a unique equilibrium for the economy E. Furthermore, for every agent h, v^h is continuously differentiable and additive separable in x^h and

(m^h, π), the $(\ell n+n+\ell) \times (\ell n+n+\ell+1)$ derivative matrix of ψ_E at $(\bar{x}, \bar{m}, \pi^*)$ denoted $D\psi_E(\bar{x}, \bar{m}, \pi^*) = (G, g)$, where $g = (g^1, \ldots, g^n, 0)'_{(\ell n+n+\ell)\times 1}$ with $g^h = ((\partial^2 v^h/\partial m^h \partial p_0)p_1, \ldots, (\partial^2 v^h/\partial m^h \partial p_0)p_\ell, 0)$, $h = 1, \ldots, n$, and

$$G = \left(\begin{array}{c|c|c|c} A^1_\pi & \cdots & 0 & B^1_0 \\ \hline \vdots & \ddots & \vdots & \vdots \\ \hline 0 & \cdots & A^n_\pi & B^n_0 \\ \hline J & & J & 0 \end{array}\right)_{(\ell n+n+\ell)\times(\ell n+n+\ell)}$$

with

$$A^h = \begin{pmatrix} \dfrac{\partial^2 v^h}{\partial x_1^h \partial x_1^h} - \left(\displaystyle\sum_{k=1}^{\ell} \dfrac{\partial^2 v^h}{\partial x_k^h \partial x_1^h} + \dfrac{\partial^2 v^h}{\partial m^h \partial x_1^h}\right) p_1, \\ \ldots, \dfrac{\partial^2 v^h}{\partial x_1^h \partial m^h} - \left(\displaystyle\sum_{k=1}^{\ell} \dfrac{\partial^2 v^h}{\partial x_k^h \partial m^h} + \dfrac{\partial^2 v^h}{\partial m^h \partial m^h}\right) p_1 \\ \cdots\cdots\cdots\cdots \\ \dfrac{\partial^2 v^h}{\partial x_\ell^h \partial x_1^h} - \left(\displaystyle\sum_{k=1}^{\ell} \dfrac{\partial^2 v^h}{\partial x_k^h \partial x_1^h} + \dfrac{\partial^2 v^h}{\partial m^h \partial x_1^h}\right) p_\ell, \\ \ldots, \dfrac{\partial^2 v^h}{\partial x_\ell^h \partial m^h} - \left(\displaystyle\sum_{k=1}^{\ell} \dfrac{\partial^2 v^h}{\partial x_k^h \partial m^h} + \dfrac{\partial^2 v^h}{\partial m^h \partial m^h}\right) p_\ell \end{pmatrix}_{\ell \times (\ell+1)}$$

$$B^h = \begin{pmatrix} -\left(\frac{\partial^2 v^h}{\partial m^h \partial p_1}\right) p_1 - \left(\sum_{k=1}^{\ell} \frac{\partial v^h}{\partial x_k^h} + \frac{\partial v^h}{\partial m^h}\right), \ldots, -\left(\frac{\partial^2 v^h}{\partial m^h \partial p_\ell}\right) p_1 \\ \cdots\cdots\cdots\cdots \\ -\left(\frac{\partial^2 v^h}{\partial m^h \partial p_1}\right) p_\ell \quad , \ldots, -\left(\frac{\partial^2 v^h}{\partial m^h \partial p_\ell}\right) p_\ell - \left(\sum_{k=1}^{\ell} \frac{\partial v^h}{\partial x_k^h} + \frac{\partial v^h}{\partial m^h}\right) \end{pmatrix}_{\ell \times \ell}$$

$h = 1, \ldots, n$,

and

$$J = \begin{pmatrix} 1, \ldots, 0, 0 \\ \cdots\cdots \\ 0, \ldots, 1, 0 \end{pmatrix}_{\ell \times (\ell+1)}$$

By Propositions 3 and 4, $D_a v^h(\bar{x}^h, \bar{m}^h, \pi^*; \gamma^h, u^h) \gg 0$, and $D_a^2 v^h(\bar{x}^h, \bar{m}^h, \pi^*; \gamma^h, u^h)$ is negative definite on the space $\{\theta \in R^{\ell+1}: D_a v^h(\bar{x}^h, \bar{m}^h, \pi^*; \gamma^h, u^h) \cdot \theta = 0\}$ for every h. Hence, we have

$$0 \neq \det \left(\begin{array}{cc:c:c:c} \tilde{A}^1 & \pi & \cdots & 0 & \tilde{B}^1 \\ \pi & 0 & & & 0 \\ \hdashline \vdots & & \ddots & \vdots & \vdots \\ \hdashline 0 & & \cdots & \begin{matrix} \tilde{A}^n & \pi \\ \pi & 0 \end{matrix} & \begin{matrix} \tilde{B}^n \\ 0 \end{matrix} \\ \hdashline \tilde{J} & & \cdots & \tilde{J} & 0 \end{array}\right)_{(\ell n+2n+\ell)\times(\ell n+2n+\ell)}$$

$$= \det \left(\begin{array}{cc:c:cc:c} A^1 & p & & & & B^1 \\ 0 & 1 & \cdots & 0 & & 0 \\ \pi & 0 & & & & 0 \\ \hdashline \vdots & & \ddots & \vdots & & \vdots \\ \hdashline & & & A^n & p & B^n \\ 0 & & \cdots & 0 & 1 & 0 \\ & & & \pi & 0 & 0 \\ \hdashline \tilde{J} & & \cdots & \tilde{J} & & 0 \end{array}\right)$$

$$= (-1) \det G \quad ,$$

where

$$\tilde{A}^h = \begin{pmatrix} \dfrac{\partial^2 v^h}{\partial x_1^h \partial x_1^h} & ,\dots, & \dfrac{\partial^2 v^h}{\partial x_1^h \partial m^h} \\ \dots\dots\dots & & \\ \dfrac{\partial^2 v^h}{\partial m^h \partial x_1^h} & ,\dots, & \dfrac{\partial^2 v^h}{\partial m^h \partial m^h} \end{pmatrix}_{(\ell+1)\times(\ell+1)}$$

$$\tilde{B}^h = \begin{pmatrix} -\sum_{k=1}^{\ell} \dfrac{\partial v^h}{\partial x_k^h} + \dfrac{\partial v^h}{\partial m^h} & ,\dots, & 0 \\ \dots\dots\dots & & \\ 0 & ,\dots, & -\sum_{k=1}^{\ell} \dfrac{\partial v^h}{\partial x_k^h} + \dfrac{\partial v^h}{\partial m^h} \\ \dfrac{\partial^2 v^h}{\partial m^h \partial p_1} + \sum_{k=1}^{\ell} \dfrac{\partial v^h}{\partial x_k^h} + \dfrac{\partial v^h}{\partial m^h} & ,\dots, & \dfrac{\partial^2 v^h}{\partial m^h \partial p_\ell} + \sum_{k=1}^{\ell} \dfrac{\partial v^h}{\partial x_k^h} + \dfrac{\partial v^h}{\partial m^h} \end{pmatrix}_{(\ell+1)\times \ell}$$

$h = 1,\dots,n$, and $\tilde{J} = (J, 0)_{\ell \times (\ell+2)}$.

Therefore, $D\psi_E(\bar{x}, \bar{m}, \pi^*)$ has rank $\ell n + n + \ell$. In other words, $E \in \mathscr{R}$. Q.E.D.

As a matter of fact, the "strong" topology defined on $\mathscr{E}$, which establishes the generic local uniqueness and stability of extended (or classical) temporary monetary equilibrium, does not make the space $\mathscr{E}$ a topological vector space since $P^n \times R^n_+ \times \Pi$ is certainly non-compact. Toward proving the existence theorem, we need the so-called "weak" topology of $\mathscr{E}$ defined by the n-fold product of the induced C^1 compact-open topology on Γ, the induced C^k compact-open topology on $\mathscr{U}$ and the induced usual topologies on P and R_+, respectively. It is obvious that the "weak" topology on $\mathscr{E}$ does not control the behavior of the maps and their derivatives "at infinity" very well, but it would make $\mathscr{E}$ metrizable. We now introduce some concepts of degree theory in differential topology. Let $f: X \to Y$ be a C^k map, where X is compact without boundary, Y is connected, and both X and Y are manifolds and have the same dimensions. If y is a regular value of f, we denote $\deg_2(f;y) = \# f^{-1}(y)$ the number of solutions x to the equation $f(x) = y$. In fact, $\deg_2(f;y)$ does not depend on the choice of the regular value y. That is, if y and z are regular values of f, then $\deg_2(f;y) = \# f^{-1}(z) = \deg_2(f;z)$. Let $\deg_2 f = \deg_2(f;y)$, for all regular values y of f. $\deg_2 f$ is called the <u>degree modulo</u> 2 of f. We say that two C^k maps $f: X \to Y$ and $g: X \to Y$ are C^k-<u>homotopic</u>, if there is a C^k map $F: X \times [0, 1] \to Y$ such that $F(x, 0) = f(x)$ and $F(x, 1) = g(x)$.

F is called a C^k-homotopy between f and g. Now, suppose that $f: X \to Y$ is C^k-homotopic to $g: X \to Y$, where X is compact and without boundary. If $y \in Y$ is a regular value for both f and g, then $\deg_2(f;y) = \# f^{-1}(y) = \# g^{-1}(y) = \deg_2(g;y)$. This claims that $\deg_2 f$ is a C^k-homotopy invariant. In order to define the degree as an integer rather than an integer modulo 2, we must introduce orientations. An orientation for a finite dimensional real vector space is an equivalence class of ordered bases as follows: the order basis $(x_1, \ldots, x_n)$ determines the same orientation as the basis $(y_1, \ldots, y_n)$ if $y_i = \Sigma_{j=1}^n a_{ij} x_j$ with $\det(a_{ij}) > 0$. It determines the opposite orientation if $\det(a_{ij}) < 0$. The Euclidean space R^n has a standard orientation corresponding to the basis $(1, 0, \ldots, 0)$, $(0, 1, 0, \ldots, 0)$, $\ldots$, $(0, \ldots, 0, 1)$. An oriented C^k-manifold consists of a manifold X and a choice of orientation for each tangent space $T_x X$ fitting together as follows: for each point of X there exists an open set $U \subset X$ and a diffeomorphism $\phi: U \to V \subset R^n$ such that for each $x \in U$, $D\phi(x): T_x X \to R^n$ carries the orientation of $T_x X$ into the standard orientation of R^n. If X can be oriented, it is said to be orientable.

Let X and Y be oriented n-dimensional manifolds without boundary and let $f: X \to Y$ be a C^k map. If X is compact and Y is connected, then the degree of f is defined as follows: Let $x \in X$ be a regular point of f so that $Df(x): T_x X \to T_{f(x)} Y$

is a linear isomorphism between oriented vector spaces. Define the sign of Df(x) to be +1 or -1 according as Df(x) preserves or reverses orientation. For any regular value $y \in Y$, we define $\deg(f;y) = \Sigma_{x \in f^{-1}(y)} \text{sign } Df(x)$. It can be shown that the integer deg (f;y) does not depend on the choice of regular value. Denote deg f = deg (f;y) for all regular values y of f. We call deg f the Brouwer degree of f. The important property of deg f is that the integer deg f is C^k-homotopy invariant, that is, if f is C^k-homotopic to $g: X \to Y$, then deg f = deg g provided X is compact and without boundary. In case X is non-compact, the above argument of degree theory holds if the functions f and g are proper.

Now, we prove an existence theorem as follows:

THEOREM 3. *There exists extended temporary monetary equilibrium for every money economy, i.e., for all* $E \in \mathscr{E}$, $\Phi(E) \neq \phi$.

Proof. First, we check $\mathscr{E}$ is arcwise connected.[12] Let $E, E' \in \mathscr{E}$. We construct $E^\tau = \tau E + (1-\tau)E'$ for $\tau \in [0, 1]$, i.e.,

$$E^\tau = (\gamma^\tau, u^\tau, \bar{x}^\tau, \bar{m}^\tau)$$

$$= (\tau\gamma + (1-\tau)\gamma', \ \tau u + (1-\tau)u', \ \tau\bar{x} + (1-\tau)\bar{x}', \ \tau\bar{m} + (1-\tau)\bar{m}')$$

12 A topological space X is said to be arcwise-connected if, for each pair of points a, b in X there exists a path in X with origin a and end point b, where a path X is a continuous function $f: [0, 1] \to X$ such that $f(0) = a$, $f(1) = b$ (see also [15]).

By the "weak" topology given on $\mathscr{E}$, $\gamma^{h\tau} \in C^1(\Pi, \mathscr{M}(\Pi \times P))$, $u^{h\tau} \in C^k(P \times P, R)$ with $k > 2$, $\bar{x}^{h\tau} \in P$ and $\bar{m}^{h\tau} \in R_+$ for every h. It is easy to see that $u^{h\tau}$ is bounded and satisfies A. 2 and A. 3. That is, $u^{h\tau} \in \mathscr{U}$. Moreover, we recall that the support of a non-negative measure (probability measure as a special case) can be written in the following form: $\text{supp}\ \gamma^h(\pi) = \{z \in \Pi \times P\colon\ \gamma^h(\pi; N) > 0$ for each open set N containing $z\}$ (see [46], Theorem 2. 1), where z is a pair of future prices and future endowments. We claim that (i) $\text{supp}\ \gamma^h(\pi) = \text{supp}\ \alpha\gamma^h(\pi)$ for $\alpha > 0$, and (ii) $\text{supp}(\gamma^h(\pi) + \gamma^{h'}(\pi)) = \text{supp}\ \gamma^h(\pi) \cup \text{supp}\ \gamma^{h'}(\pi)$ for any $\pi \in \Pi$. (i) is clear. If $z \in \text{supp}(\gamma^h(\pi) + \gamma^{h'}(\pi))$, $\gamma^h(\pi; N) + \gamma^{h'}(\pi; N) > 0$ for every open set N containing z. That is, we have either $\gamma^h(\pi; N) > 0$ or $\gamma^{h'}(\pi; N) > 0$ for every open set N containing z. This implies $z \in \text{supp}\ \gamma^h(\pi) \cup \text{supp}\ \gamma^{h'}(\pi)$. Therefore, $\text{supp}(\gamma^h(\pi) + \gamma^{h'}(\pi)) \subset \text{supp}\ \gamma^h(\pi) \cup \text{supp}\ \gamma^{h'}(\pi)$ for any $\pi \in \Pi$. On the other hand, since $\gamma^h(\pi) \geq 0$ and $\gamma^{h'}(\pi) \geq 0$, $\gamma^h(\pi) \leq \gamma^h(\pi) + \gamma^{h'}(\pi)$ and $\gamma^{h'}(\pi) \leq \gamma^h(\pi) + \gamma^{h'}(\pi)$. By definition of the support of a measure, we have $\text{supp}\ \gamma^h(\pi) \cup \text{supp}\ \gamma^{h'}(\pi) \subset \text{supp}(\gamma^h(\pi) + \gamma^{h'}(\pi))$ for any $\pi \in \Pi$. We recall that $\gamma^{h\tau} = \tau\gamma^h + (1-\tau)\gamma^{h'}$ with $\tau \in [0, 1]$. If $\tau = 0$, then $\gamma^{h\tau} = \gamma^{h'}$ and $\text{supp}\ \gamma^{h\tau}(\pi) = \text{supp}\ \gamma^{h'}(\pi)$ for any $\pi \in \Pi$. Similarly, if $\tau = 1$, $\text{supp}\ \gamma^{h\tau}(\pi) = \text{supp}\ \gamma^h(\pi)$ for any $\pi \in \Pi$. If $0 < \tau < 1$,

$$\begin{aligned}\operatorname{supp} \gamma^{h\tau}(\pi) &= \operatorname{supp}(\tau\gamma^{h}(\pi) + (1-\tau)\gamma^{h'}(\pi)) \\ &= \operatorname{supp} \tau\gamma^{h}(\pi) + \operatorname{supp}(1-\tau)\gamma^{h'}(\pi) \\ &= \operatorname{supp} \gamma^{h}(\pi) \cup \operatorname{supp} \gamma^{h'}(\pi)\end{aligned}$$

for any $\pi \in \Pi$. Since $\gamma^{h}, \gamma^{h'} \in \Gamma$ for every agent h, $\operatorname{supp} \gamma^{h}(\pi)$ and $\operatorname{supp} \gamma^{h'}(\pi)$ are compact for any $\pi \in \Pi$. Hence $\operatorname{supp} \gamma^{h\tau}(\pi)$ is a compact set in $\Pi \times P$ for $\pi \in \Pi$ and $\tau \in [0, 1]$. In other words, $\gamma^{h\tau} \in \Gamma$. This proves that $E^{\tau} = (\gamma^{\tau}, u^{\tau}, \bar{x}^{\tau}, \bar{m}^{\tau}) \in \mathscr{E}$. Now, consider the map $\psi_E: P^n \times R^n_+ \times \Pi \to R^{\ell n+n+\ell}$ defined by (5). By Proposition 5, ψ_E is proper. In particular, $\psi_E^{-1}(0)$ is compact and boundaryless in $P^n \times R^n_+ \times \Pi$. Therefore, the Brouwer degree of the map ψ_E is defined. If $E \in \mathscr{R}$, the degree of the map ψ_E is equal to the algebraic sum of the orientations of the elements of $\psi_E^{-1}(0)$. Let $\deg \psi_E$ denote the degree of map ψ_E. By Proposition 7, there exists $E \in \mathscr{R} \subset \mathscr{E}$, $\deg \psi_E$ is one. Finally, the Brouwer degree is homotopy invariant, so that $\deg \psi_E$ is one for every $E \in \mathscr{E}$. This implies $\psi_E^{-1}(0) \neq \phi$ and hence $\Phi(E) = \psi_E^{-1}(0) \neq \phi$ for every $E \in \mathscr{E}$. Q. E. D.

COROLLARY 3. <u>For every classical money economy, there is a temporary monetary equilibrium</u>, <u>i. e.</u>, $W(E) \neq \phi$ <u>for all</u> $E \in \mathscr{E}_0$.

Remark 2. It is obvious from the definition of Brouwer degree, $\Phi(E)$ and $W(E)$ have an odd number of elements for every $E \in \mathscr{R}$ and $E \in \mathscr{R}_0$, respectively. In particular, if the sign of the determinant of the non-singular $(\ell n+n+\ell) \times (\ell n+n+\ell)$ sub-matrix of the derivatives of ψ_E at (x, m, π) were constant for every $(x, m, \pi) \in \psi_E^{-1}(0)$, there is only one extended or classical temporary monetary equilibrium for E in $\mathscr{E}$ or $\mathscr{E}_0$.

Chapter V

AN EXTENSION - TEMPORARY MONETARY EQUILIBRIUM THEORY WITH SPOT AND FUTURES TRANSACTIONS

In this chapter, one extends the results of previous studies on temporary "spot" monetary equilibrium to the case of allowing sequential trading of commodities and money in both present and future. In other words, markets are open at every date. As discussed earlier, in a temporary equilibrium analysis, the agent's expectations of future environment link the subsequent markets together and it becomes very natural to introduce money and futures contracts in the sense that the exchange of present commodities or ready money for a promise to deliver commodities and money in the future is permitted in the model. The existence of both spot markets and futures contracts derives the possibility of speculation in the markets. As pointed out by Hicks, "no forward market can do without the speculative element" [32], and this idea is well applicable in the theory of foreign trade.

The formal model of this type was studied by Green in [27], and it is restricted to the pure exchange non-monetary economy. Moreover, an extension [28] has been made in the direction of allowing bankruptcy with some probability and of agents which can also be endowed with preexisting contracts when the market of the current period opens. This chapter shows that "models of this type will provide a framework for the study of monetary theory" [28]. In particular, in a money economy, the presence of spot and futures transactions explains at least in part the precautionary and speculative motives of money holding provided that money is the only store of value between periods and is associated with no direct utility. A further suggestive interpretation of the model is that there are separate markets, or trading posts, one for each commodity other than money, where the agents exchange each commodity for money simultaneously at the ruling prices (this is possible due to the inconvenience of barter in reality). Thus, money plays the role of "medium of exchange" in the formulation and hence the transactive demand of money is revealed explicitly. However, all the results obtained in this chapter certainly are not dependent on this particular interpretation of the model.

Section V(a) presents the model. In Section V(b), we prove analogous properties on the structure of the set of temporary monetary equilibria with spot and futures transactions, as those in Chapter IV. Accordingly, the set of temporary monetary equilibria in such markets is locally unique and depends continuously on the economy. A compactness argument and some degree of compatibility on expectations among agents which are usually assumed for this type model (see [27] for instance) are also employed in this chapter.

V(a) The Model

As in Chapter II, suppose for simplicity there are two periods t and $t+1$ and for each period, there are ℓ (perishable) commodities indexed by $i(i=1,\ldots,\ell)$, and n agents indexed by $h(h=1,\ldots,n)$. Physically, for periods t and $t+1$, there are ℓ identical commodities[13] and the storage of these commodities is impossible. Money links successive periods as the only store of value, which affords no direct utility. In period t, there are markets for the ℓ currently deliverable commodities and markets for contracts of future delivery of the same commodities. It is clear that agents are also allowed to engage in money transactions. For example, they can exchange present commodities and ready money for promises to pay money in the future, or vice versa. Hence, various loan transactions may occur by trading commodities and money in the future against present ones. In this sense, spot markets will be active in both periods t and $t+1$, and spot prices at $t+1$ will in general differ from prices for future contracts in period t. Let

---

[13] Again, this is assumed only for notational convenience and is not necessary to carry out the analysis (see, for instance [27]).

$$\Pi^t = \left\{ \pi^t = (p^t, p_0^t, q^t, q_0^t) \in R^{2(\ell+1)} : \pi^t >> 0 \quad \text{and} \quad \sum_{i=1}^{\ell} p_i^t + p_0^t + \sum_{i=1}^{\ell} q_i^t + q_0^t = 1 \right\}$$

be the price space at time t, where π^t consists of the spot prices (p^t, p_0^t) of currently deliverable commodities and money, and the prices (q^t, q_0^t) of future contracts. Since there are no active future markets at time $t+1$, the price space of period $t+1$ is simply

$$\Pi^{t+1} = \left\{ \pi^{t+1} = (p^{t+1}, p_0^{t+1}) \in R^{\ell+1} : \pi^{t+1} >> 0 \quad \text{and} \quad \sum_{i=1}^{\ell} p_i^{t+1} + p_0^{t+1} = 1 \right\} .$$

Let P be the consumption space for every agent at each period, and the pair $(x^{ht}, x^{ht+1}) \in P \times P$ is the consumption stream of agent h over two periods t and $t+1$. Suppose R_+ to be the money space of any agent at each period, and $m^{ht} \in R_+$ denotes the h-th agent's money holding at time t. An action of agent h at time t is a triple of current consumption, money holding, and future contract, denoted $(x^{ht}, m^{ht}, f^{ht}) \in P \times R_+ \times R^{\ell+1}$ where $f^{ht} = (b^{ht}, c^{ht}) \in R^{\ell} \times R$. If $b_i^{ht} > 0$ (resp. $c^{ht} > 0$), the h-th agent has contracted at time t for the delivery of b_i^{ht} (resp., c^{ht}) units of commodity i (resp., money) at time $t+1$, and conversely. We define $\mathscr{E} = (\Gamma \times \mathscr{U} \times P \times R_+)^n$ to be the space of money economies with spot and futures contracts at period t, and a money economy $E = (\gamma, u, \bar{x}^t, \bar{m}^t) \in \mathscr{E}$ where $\gamma = (\gamma^1, \ldots, \gamma^n)$, $u = (u^1, \ldots, u^n)$, $\bar{x}^t = (\bar{x}^{1t}, \ldots, \bar{x}^{nt})$ and $\bar{m}^{1t}, \ldots, \bar{m}^{nt})$. For a special case, $\mathscr{E}_0 = (\Gamma \times \mathscr{U}_0 \times P \times R_+)^n$ is a space of classical money economies with spot and futures contracts at time t. The notation is explained further in the following:

(a) $(\bar{x}^{ht}, \bar{m}^{ht}) \in P \times R_+$, the initial commodity and money endowments of agent h at time t, which is known with certainty at the beginning of period t. Assume $\Sigma_{h=1}^n \bar{m}^{ht} > 0$.

(b) $\Gamma = \Big\{ \gamma^h \in C^1(\Pi^t, \mathscr{M}(\Pi^{t+1} \times P))$: (i) supp $\gamma^h(\pi^t)$ is compact in $\Pi^{t+1} \times P$, and it is independent of the choice of $\pi^t \in \Pi^t$. (ii) $(q^t/\Sigma_{i=1}^{\ell} q_i^t + q_0^t, \; q_0^t/\Sigma_{i=1}^{\ell} q_i^t + q_0^t) \in$ int co $\text{supp}_1\, \gamma^h(\pi^t)$ for each $\pi^t \in \Pi^t$, where $(q^t/\Sigma_{i=1}^{\ell} q_i^t + q_0^t, q_0^t/\Sigma_{i=1}^{\ell} q_i^t + q_0^t)$ is the vector of relative prices of forward contracts and int co $\text{supp}_1\, \gamma^h(\pi^t)$ is the interior of the convex hull of the projection of supp $\gamma^h(\pi^t)$ on Π^{t+1}. (iii) $\bigcap_{h=1}^n$ int co $\text{supp}_1\, \gamma^h(\pi^t) \neq \phi$ for each $\pi^t \in \Pi^t \Big\}$

is called the space of expectation functions for every agent, where γ^h specifies a subjective uncertainty about the future price system $\pi^{t+1} = (p^{t+1}, p_0^{t+1}) \in \Pi^{t+1}$ and future commodity endowment $\bar{x}^{ht+1} \in P$ conditional to a current price system $\pi^t = (p^t, p_0^t, q^t, q_0^t) \in \Pi^t$. In (i), the independence of $\operatorname{supp} \gamma^h(\pi^t)$ with respect to $\pi^t \in \Pi^t$ can be replaced by some weaker assumptions but with a cost of complicating the exposition of the analysis (see for example [27]). In fact, (i) is a very reasonable restriction on the expectations, especially in a normal and stable economy. That is, although the agent's expectation pattern is allowed to change, there are some future events which always assign a positive weight in his/her various beliefs. (ii) claims that there must be genuine uncertainty about the future spot prices, and (iii) says that in spite of the existence of price uncertainty, there exists some agreement among agents on the expectations of future price systems.

(c) $\mathcal{U} = \{u^h \in C^k(P \times P, R) : k > 2,$ u^h is bounded and satisfies (i) $u^{h^{-1}}(c) \subset P \times P$ for any $c \in R$,

(ii) $D u^h(x^{ht}, x^{ht+1}) = (D_{x^{ht}} u^h(x^{ht}, x^{ht+1}), D_{x^{ht+1}} u^h(x^{ht}, x^{ht+1}))$ $\gg 0$, and $D^2_{x^{ht+1}} u^h(x^{ht}, x^{ht+1})$ is negative definite on the space $\{\mu \in R^\ell : D_{x^{ht+1}} u^h(x^{ht}, x^{ht+1}) \cdot \mu = 0\}$ for every $(x^{ht}, x^{ht+1}) \in P \times P\}$

is called the space of direct utility functions for every agent, and the space of concave direct utility functions for every agent is defined as the following:

(d) $\mathcal{U}_0 = \{u^h \in \mathcal{U} : D^2u^h(x^{ht}, x^{ht+1})$ is negative definite on the space $\{\xi \in R^{2\ell} : Du^h(x^{ht}, x^{ht+1}) \cdot \xi = 0\}$ for every $(x^{ht}, x^{ht+1}) \in P \times P\}$.

For any $u^h \in \mathcal{U}$ and $\gamma^h \in \Gamma$, a future consumption plan associated with an action (x^{ht}, m^{ht}, f^{ht}) and an expectation of future event $(\pi^{t+1}, \bar{x}^{ht+1})$ is defined by the set

$$\hat{x}^{ht+1}(x^{ht}, m^{ht}, f^{ht}; \pi^{t+1}, \bar{x}^{ht+1})$$

$$= \{x^{ht+1} \in P : u^{ht}(x^{ht}, x^{ht+1}) \text{ is maximized subject to}$$

$$p^{t+1} \cdot x^{ht+1} = p^{t+1} \cdot (\bar{x}^{ht+1} + b^{ht}) + p_0^{t+1} \cdot (m^{ht} + c^{ht})\}.$$

It is clear that $\hat{x}^{ht+1}$ is well defined on $P \times R_+ \times F^h \times K^h$, where $K^h = \text{supp}\, \gamma^h(\pi^t)$ for any $\pi^t \in \Pi^t$, and

$$F^h = \{f^{ht} = (b^{ht}, c^{ht}) \in R^\ell \times R : p^{t+1} \cdot (\bar{x}^{ht+1} + b^{ht})$$

$$+ p_0^{t+1} \cdot (m^{ht} + c^{ht}) > 0 \quad \text{for all } (\pi^{t+1}, \bar{x}^{ht+1}) \in K^h\}.$$

Although each agent is permitted to engage in future contracts in excess of initial commodity and money endowments, the set F^h restrains agents from bankruptcy even with a small positive probability in period t+1. At time t, if $\pi^t = (p^t, p_0^t, q^t, q_0^t) \in \Pi^t$ is the prevailing price system, the h-th agent's expected utility function can be derived from a dynamical programming process discussed in Chapter II. That is,

$$v^h(x^{ht}, m^{ht}, f^{ht}, \pi^t; \gamma^h, u^h) = \int_{\Pi^{t+1} \times P} \hat{u}^h(x^{ht}, m^{ht}, f^{ht}; \cdot, \cdot)\, d\gamma^h(\pi^t; \cdot, \cdot)$$

where

$$\hat{u}^h(x^{ht}, m^{ht}, f^{ht}; \pi^{t+1}, \bar{x}^{t+1}) = u^h(x^{ht}, \hat{x}^{ht+1}(x^{ht}, m^{ht}, f^{ht}; \pi^{t+1}, \bar{x}^{ht+1}))$$

provided that the consumption plan $\hat{x}^{ht+1}$ is well defined. In the following, we shall drop the time index t and let $(\tilde{\pi}, \tilde{\bar{x}}^h) = (\pi^{t+1}, \bar{x}^{ht+1})$ and $\tilde{\Pi} = \Pi^{t+1}$ for convenience. It is clear that the expected utility function v^h depends on the current action $(x^h, m^h, f^h) \in P \times R_+ \times F^h$ and price system $\pi \in \Pi$ as well as the economic data $(\gamma^h, u^h) \in \Gamma \times \mathcal{U}$. It is obvious that we have the following:

PROPOSITION 8. <u>For each agent</u> h, $v^h(\cdot, \cdot, \cdot, \cdot; \gamma^h, u^h) \in C^1(P \times R_+ \times F^h \times \Pi, R)$ <u>for each</u> $\gamma^h \in \Gamma$ <u>and</u> $u^h \in \mathcal{U}$. <u>In</u>

<u>particular,</u> $v^h(\cdot\,,\cdot\,,\cdot\,,\pi;\gamma^h,u^h) \in C^{k-1}(P \times R_+ \times F^h, R)$ <u>with</u> $k > 2$ <u>for each</u> $\pi \in \Pi$.

<u>Proof.</u> See Propositions 1 and 2.

Let

$$\begin{aligned}
D_1 v^h(x^h, m^h, f^h, \pi; \gamma^h, u^h) &= (\partial v^h(x^h, m^h, f^h, \pi; \gamma^h, u^h)/\partial x_1^h, \ldots, \\
&\quad \partial v^h(x^h, m^h, f^h, \pi; \gamma^h, u^h)/\partial x_\ell^h) ,
\end{aligned}$$

$$D_2 v^h(x^h, m^h, f^h, \pi; \gamma^h, u^h) = \partial v^h(x^h, m^h, f^h, \pi; g^h, u^h)/\partial m^h ,$$

$$\begin{aligned}
D_b v^h(x^h, m^h, f^h, \pi; \gamma^h, u^h) &= (\partial v^h(x^h, m^h, f^h, \pi; \gamma^h, u^h)/\partial b_1^h, \ldots, \\
&\quad \partial v^h(x^h, m^h, f^h, \pi; \gamma^h, u^h)/\partial b_\ell^h) ,
\end{aligned}$$

$$D_c v^h(x^h, m^h, f^h, \pi; \gamma^h, u^h) = \partial v^h(x^h, m^h, f^h, \pi; \gamma^h, u^h)/\partial c^h ,$$

and

$$\begin{aligned}
D_3 v^h(x^h, m^h, f^h, \pi; \gamma^h, u^h) &= (D_b v^h(x^h, m^h, f^h, \pi; \gamma^h, u^h) , \\
&\quad D_c v^h(x^h, m^h, f^h, \pi; \gamma^h, u^h)) ,
\end{aligned}$$

$$\begin{aligned}
D_a v^h(x^h, m^h, f^h, \pi; \gamma^h, u^h) &= (D_1 v^h(x^h, m^h, f^h, \pi; \gamma^h, u^h), \\
&\quad D_2 v^h(x^h, m^h, f^h, \pi; \gamma^h, u^h), \\
&\quad D_3 v^h(x^h, m^h, f^h, \pi; \gamma^h, u^h)) .
\end{aligned}$$

In analogy with the Propositions 3 and 4, we establish the following properties on the expected utility functions:

PROPOSITION 9. For each agent h

$$\overline{v^h(\cdot, m^h, f^h, \pi; \gamma^h, u^h)^{-1}(c)} \subset P \quad \text{for any } c \in R, \text{ and}$$

$$D_a v^h(x^h, m^h, f^h, \pi; \gamma^h, u^h) = \Big(\int_{\Pi \times P} D_{x^h} \hat{u}^h(x^h, m^h, f^h; \cdot, \cdot)\, d\gamma^h(\pi; \cdot, \cdot),$$

$$\int_{\Pi \times P} D_{m^h} \hat{u}^h(x^h, m^h, f^h; \cdot, \cdot)\, d\gamma^h(\pi; \cdot, \cdot),$$

$$\int_{\Pi \times P} D_{f^h} \hat{u}^h(x^h, m^h, f^h; \cdot, \cdot)\, d\gamma^h(\pi; \cdot, \cdot) \Big)$$

$$\gg 0$$

for each $(x^h, m^h, f^h, \pi) \in P \times R_+ \times F^h \times \Pi$ and $(\gamma^h, u^h) \in \Gamma \times \mathcal{U}$.

PROPOSITION 10. Given $\pi \in \Pi$, if v^h is induced by $u^h \in \mathcal{U}_0$ and $\gamma^h \in \Gamma$, $v^h(\cdot, \cdot, \cdot, \pi; \gamma^h, u^h)$ is a differentiably concave C^{k-1} function from $P \times R_+ \times F^h$ to R with $k > 2$. That is, there exists $\theta \in R^{2(\ell+1)}$ such that $D_a^2 v^h(x^h, m^h, f^h, \pi; \gamma^h, u^h)$ is negative definite on the space $\{\theta \in R^{2(\ell+1)} : D_a v^h(x^h, m^h, f^h, \pi; \gamma^h, u^h) \cdot \theta = 0\}$ for every $(x^h, m^h, f^h) \in P \times R_+ \times F^h$.

As usual, a temporary monetary equilibrium for an economy $E = (\gamma, u, \bar{x}, \bar{m}) \in \mathscr{E}$ at the current period is a quadruple $(x, m, f, \pi) \in P^n \times R^n_+ \times F \times \Pi$, where $x = (x^1, \ldots, x^n)$, $m = (m^1, \ldots, m^n)$, $f = (f^1, \ldots, f^n)$ and $F = F^1 \times \cdots \times F^n$, with $\Sigma^n_{h=1} x^h = \Sigma^n_{h=1} \bar{x}^h$, $\Sigma^n_{h=1} m^h = \Sigma^n_{h=1} \bar{m}^h$, $\Sigma^n_{h=1} f^h = 0$, and satisfying $p \cdot x^h + p_0 \cdot m^h + q \cdot b^h + q_0 \cdot c^h = p \cdot \bar{x}^h + p_0 \cdot \bar{m}^h$ for every h and that $v^h(x^h, m^h, f^h, \pi; \gamma^h, u^h)$ is maximized for every agent h. For any h, the Lagrangian condition for (x^h, m^h, f^h) to be a critical point of $v^h(\cdot, \cdot, \cdot, \pi; \gamma^h, u^h)$ subject to $p \cdot x^h + p_0 \cdot m^h + q \cdot b^h + q_0 \cdot c^h = p \cdot \bar{x}^h + p_0 \cdot \bar{m}^h$ can be written as $D_a v^h(x^h, m^h, f^h, \pi; \gamma^h, u^h) = \lambda^h \cdot \pi$, where λ^h is the Lagrangian multiplier. To avoid λ^h in the model, we set

$$\lambda^h = |D_a v^h(x^h, m^h, f^h, \pi; \gamma^h, u^h)|$$

where

$$\begin{aligned} |D_a v^h(x^h, m^h, f^h, \pi; \gamma^h, u^h)| = & \sum_{i=1}^{\ell} \partial v^h(x^h, m^h, f^h, \pi; \gamma^h, u^h)/\partial x^h_i \\ & + \partial v^h(x^h, m^h, f^h, \pi; \gamma^h, u^h)/\partial m^h \\ & + \sum_{i=1}^{\ell} \partial v^h(x^h, m^h, f^h, \pi; \gamma^h, u^h)/\partial b^h_i \\ & + \partial v^h(x^h, m^h, f^h, \pi; \gamma^h, u^h)/\partial c^h \ . \end{aligned}$$

From Proposition 9, it is obvious that $\lambda^h > 0$ for every h. Let W(E) be the set of (classical) temporary monetary equilibria for $E \in \mathscr{E}$, that is,

$$W(E) = \Big\{ (x, m, f, \pi) \in P^n \times R_+^n \times F \times \Pi : v^h(x^h, m^h, f^h, \pi; \gamma^h, u^h)$$

$$\text{is maximized, } p \cdot x^h + p_0 \cdot m^h + q \cdot b^h + q_0 \cdot c^h$$

$$= p \cdot \bar{x}^h + p_0 \cdot \bar{m}^h, \ h = 1, \ldots, n, \ \sum_{h=1}^n x^h = \sum_{h=1}^n \bar{x}^h,$$

$$\sum_{h=1}^n m^h = \sum_{h=1}^n \bar{m}^h, \text{ and } \sum_{h=1}^n f^h = 0 \Big\} .$$

Similarly, the set of extended temporary monetary equilibria for $E \in \mathscr{E}$ is

$$\Phi(E) = \Big\{ (x, m, f, \pi) \in P^n \times R_+^n \times F \times \Pi : D_a v^h(x^h, m^h, f^h, \pi; \gamma^h, u^h)$$

$$= |D_a v^h(x^h, m^h, f^h, \pi; \gamma^h, u^h)| \cdot \pi, \ p \cdot x^h + p_0 \cdot m^h + q \cdot b^h + q_0 \cdot c^h$$

$$= p \cdot \bar{x}^h + p_0 \cdot \bar{m}^h, \ h = 1, \ldots, n, \ \sum_{h=1}^n x^h = \sum_{h=1}^n \bar{x}^h,$$

$$\sum_{h=1}^n m^h = \sum_{h=1}^n \bar{m}^h, \text{ and } \sum_{h=1}^n f^h = 0 \Big\} .$$

For every money economy $E \in \mathscr{E}$, we now define a C^1 map $\psi_E : P^n \times R_+^n \times F \times \Pi \to R^{(2\ell+1)n+n+(2\ell+1)}$ with the form

$$\psi_E(x, m, f, \pi) = \Big(D_1 v^h(x^h, m^h, f^h, \pi; \gamma^h, u^h) - |D_a v^h(x^h, m^h, f^h, \pi; \gamma^h, u^h)| \cdot p,$$

$$D_b v^h(x^h, m^h, f^h, \pi; \gamma^h, u^h) - |D_a v^h(x^h, m^h, f^h, \pi; \gamma^h, u^h)| \cdot q,$$

$$D_c v^h(x^h, m^h, f^h, \pi; \gamma^h, u^h) - |D_a v^h(x^h, m^h, f^h, \pi; \gamma^h, u^h)| \cdot q_0,$$

$$p \cdot x^h + p_0 \cdot m^h + q \cdot b^h + q_0 \cdot c^h - p \cdot \bar{x}^h - p_0 \cdot \bar{m}^h, \quad h = 1, \ldots, n,$$

$$\sum_{h=1}^{n} x^h - \sum_{h=1}^{n} \bar{x}^h, \ \sum_{h=1}^{n} f^h \Big) .$$

Since the conditions

$$\sum_{h=1}^{n} m^h = \sum_{h=1}^{n} \bar{m}^h$$

and

$$D_2 v^h(x^h, m^h, f^h, \pi; \gamma^h, u^h) - |D_a v^h(x^h, m^h, f^h, \pi; \gamma^h, u^h)| \cdot p_0$$

can be obtained from the others and

$$\sum_{i=1}^{\ell} p_i + p_0 + \sum_{i=1}^{\ell} q_i + q_0 = 1 \quad ,$$

it is easy to see that $\Phi(E) = \psi_E^{-1}(0)$ for every money economy $E \in \mathscr{E}$. Now, we show the following:

PROPOSITION 11. <u>The map</u> $\psi_E : P^n \times R_+^n \times F \times \Pi \to R^{(2\ell+1)n+n+(2\ell+1)}$ <u>defined as above is proper for every</u> $E \in \mathscr{E}$. <u>In particular</u> $\Phi(E)$ <u>is a compact subset in</u> $P^n \times R_+^n \times F \times \Pi$ <u>for every</u> $E \in \mathscr{E}$.

Proof. We shall prove the second half of the statement, which can be generalized to the properness of the map ψ_E for every $E \in \mathscr{E}$. Since $\Phi(E) = \psi_E^{-1}(0)$ for every $E \in \mathscr{E}$ and ψ_E is class C^1, $\Phi(E)$ is closed in $P^n \times R_+^n \times F \times \Pi$. Moreover, if $(x, m, f, \pi) \in \Phi(E)$, x and π will not take values on the boundary of the closure of P^n and Π, respectively (see Proposition 5). By definitions of Γ and $\mathscr{U}$, the projection of the set $\Phi(E)$ along (x, m, π) in $P^n \times R_+^n \times \Pi$ is clearly bounded for every $E \in \mathscr{E}$. We need to check that the projection of $\Phi(E)$ along f in F is also bounded for every $E \in \mathscr{E}$. From the definition of Γ, supp $\gamma^h(\pi)$ is independent of $\pi \in \Pi$ and $\bigcap_{h=1}^n$ int co $\text{supp}_1\, \gamma^h(\pi) \neq \phi$. We have

$$\bigcap_{h=1}^{n} \left\{ \pi \in \Pi : \left(q/\sum_{i=1}^{\ell} q_i + q_0,\ q_0/\sum_{i=1}^{\ell} q_i + q_0 \right) \in \text{int co } \text{supp}_1\, \gamma^h(\pi) \right\} \neq \phi,$$

or

$$\left\{ \pi \in \Pi : \left(q/\sum_{i=1}^{\ell} q_i + q_0,\ q_0/\sum_{i=1}^{\ell} q_i + q_0 \right) \in \text{int co } \text{supp}_1\, \gamma^h(\pi) \right\} \neq \phi$$

for every h. By definition of $\Phi(E)$, we have the equality $p \cdot x^h + p_0 \cdot m^h + q \cdot b^h + q_0 \cdot c^h = p \cdot \bar{x}^h + p_0 \cdot \bar{m}^h$ for every $(x, m, f, \pi) \in \Phi(E)$. In other words, $q \cdot b^h + q_0 \cdot c^h < p \cdot \bar{x}^h + p_0 \cdot \bar{m}^h$ or

$$\left(q/\sum_{i=1}^{\ell} q_i + q_0 \right) \cdot b^h + \left(q_0/\sum_{i=1}^{\ell} q_i + q_0 \right) \cdot c^h < \left(p/\sum_{i=1}^{\ell} q_i + q_0 \right) \cdot \bar{x}^h + \left(p_0/\sum_{i=1}^{\ell} q_i + q_0 \right) \cdot \bar{m}^h$$

for every $(x, m, f, \pi) \in \Phi(E)$. On the other hand, since

$f^h = (b^h, c^h) \in F^h$ we have $\widetilde{p} \cdot (\widetilde{\widetilde{x}}^h + b^h) + \widetilde{p}_0 \cdot (m^h + c^h) > 0$ for any $(\widetilde{\pi}, \widetilde{\widetilde{x}}^h) \in \text{supp}\ \gamma^h(\pi)$. This inequality is also true for $\widetilde{\pi} \in$ int co $\text{supp}_1\ \gamma^h(\pi)$. Therefore, in particular,

$$- \left(\left(q / \sum_{i=1}^{\ell} q_i + q_0 \right) \cdot \widetilde{\widetilde{x}}^h + \left(q_0 / \sum_{i=1}^{\ell} q_i + q_0 \right) \cdot \ m^h \right)$$

$$< \left(q / \sum_{i=1}^{\ell} q_i + q_0 \right) \cdot b^h + \left(q_0 / \sum_{i=1}^{\ell} q_i + q_0 \right) \cdot c^h.$$

Since $\pi = (p, p_0, q, q_0) \in \Pi$, this proves that F^h is bounded for every h, and hence the projection of $\Phi(E)$ on F is bounded for every $E \in \mathscr{E}$. Moreover, if $(x, m, f, \pi) \in \Phi(E)$, $f^h = (b^h, c^h)$ will not take values on the boundary of the closure of F^h for every h. Suppose contrary, then $\widetilde{p} \cdot (\widetilde{\widetilde{x}}^h + b^h) + \widetilde{p}_0 \cdot (m^h + c^h) = 0$ for all $(\widetilde{\pi}, \widetilde{\widetilde{x}}^h) \in \text{supp}\ \gamma^h(\pi)$, and then one must eventually violate the boundary assumption (i) in the definition of $\mathscr{U}$.

Q. E. D.

V(b) Main Theorems

We first recall a few definitions. An element $E \in \mathscr{E}$ is called a regular money economy if and only if the associated map ψ_E is transversal to the origin, i. e. $\psi_E \pitchfork 0$. The space of regular money economies is denoted by $\mathscr{R} = \{E \in \mathscr{E} : \psi_E \pitchfork 0\}$

and the space of classical regular money economies is $\mathscr{R}_0 = \mathscr{R} \cap \mathscr{E}_0$. It is clear that $\psi_E^{-1}(0) = \Phi(E)$ is a C^1 submanifold of $P^n \times R_+^n \times F \times \Xi$ for every $E \in \mathscr{R}$. Following from the proof of Proposition 5, we have

PROPOSITION 12. *$\mathscr{R}$ is open and dense in $\mathscr{E}$ with respect to the "strong" topology.*

Hence two main theorems and their corollaries follow directly:

THEOREM 4. *The extended temporary monetary equilibrium $\Phi(E)$ is stable for every $E \in \mathscr{R}$ with respect to the "strong" topology.*

COROLLARY 4. *The temporary monetary equilibrium $W(E)$ is stable for every $E \in \mathscr{R}_0$ with respect to the "strong" topology.*

THEOREM 5. *For every regular money economy with spot and futures transactions, i.e., $E \in \mathscr{R}$, the set of extended temporary monetary equilibria $\Phi(E)$ is locally unique.*

COROLLARY 5. *For every regular money economy with spot and futures transactions, i.e., $E \in \mathscr{R}$, the set of temporary monetary equilibria $W(E)$ is locally unique.*

Remark 3. For Theorems 4, 5 and their corollaries to hold, there is no need to assume boundary condition on utilities for every agent and any kind of compatibility of expectations across agents. See also Remark 1 and compare.

For proving the existence of temporary monetary equilibrium for every money economy with spot and futures transactions, we need to construct a regular classical money economy which has unique temporary equilibrium, and then apply degree theory of differential topology to ensure the existence of temporary monetary equilibrium for every economies.

PROPOSITION 13. There exists a classical regular money economy with spot and futures transactions, which has unique temporary equilibrium.

Proof. Let $\mathcal{U}_{00} = \{u^h \in \mathcal{U}_0 : u^h$ is interperiod additive separable$\}$ and $\Gamma_0 = \{\gamma^h \in \Gamma : \gamma^h$ is independent of the prices of futures contracts$\}$ for every agent h. We define $\mathscr{E}_{00} = (\Gamma_0 \times \mathcal{U}_{00} \times P \times R_+)^n$, and it is clear that $\mathscr{E}_{00} \subset \mathscr{E}_0 \subset \mathscr{E}$. For an $E = (\gamma, u, \bar{x}, \bar{m}) \in \mathscr{E}_{00}$, let $(\bar{x}, \bar{m}, 0)$ be an equilibrium allocation. (In fact, this is possible if we choose $E = (\gamma, u, \bar{x}, \bar{m})$ with $\gamma^1 = \cdots = \gamma^n$, $u^1 = \cdots = u^n$, $\bar{x}^1 = \cdots = \bar{x}^n$, and $\bar{m}^1 = \cdots \bar{m}^n$.) Then there exists a unique price system $\pi^* \in \Pi$ such that $\psi_E(\bar{x}, \bar{m}, 0, \pi^*) = 0$ since $\gamma^h \in \Gamma$ and $u^h \in \mathcal{U}_0$

for every h. Because $u^h \in \mathscr{U}_{00}$, v^h is differentiably concave (Proposition 10) and additive separable with respect to x^h and (m^h, f^h, π). Furthermore, v^h is independent of the prices of future contracts because by definition $\gamma^h \in \Gamma_0$. From a well known result of consumer theory on convex preferences or concave utilities (see [49]), $p^* \cdot x^h + p_0^* m^h + q^* \cdot b^h + q_0^* \cdot c^h >$ $p^* \cdot \bar{x}^h + p_0^* \cdot \bar{m}^h$ with $(\bar{x}^h, \bar{m}^h, 0) \neq (x^h, m^h, f^h)$ for every h and $\psi_E(x, m, f, \pi^*) = 0$. This is selfcontradictory. Hence $(\bar{x}, \bar{m}, 0, \pi^*)$ is the unique equilibrium for the economy E. Moreover, the derivative matrix of ψ_E has rank $(2\ell+1)n + n + (2\ell+1)$ at $(\bar{x}, \bar{m}, 0, \pi^*)$. This follows from the facts that for every agent h, (i) v^h is additive separable in x^h and (m^h, f^h, π) and v^h is also indepêndent of (q, q_0), (ii) $D_a v^h(\bar{x}^h, \bar{m}^h, 0, \pi^*; \gamma^h, u^h) >> 0$, and (iii) $D_a^2 v^h(\bar{x}^h, \bar{m}^h, 0, \pi^*; \gamma^h, u^h)$ is negative definite on the space $\{\theta \in R^{2(\ell+1)} : D_a v^h(\bar{x}^h, \bar{m}^h, 0, \pi^*; \gamma^h, u^h) \cdot \theta = 0\}$ (for computation details, we refer to Proposition 7). Hence $E = (\gamma, u, \bar{x}, \bar{m}) \in \mathscr{R}$. Q. E. D.

THEOREM 6. <u>There exists extended temporary monetary equilibrium for every money economy with spot and futures transactions, i.e., for all</u> $E \in \mathscr{E}$, $\Phi(E) \neq \phi$.

<u>Proof.</u> As usual, we first check that $\mathscr{E}$ is arcwise connected with respect to the "weak" topology. Let $E, E' \in \mathscr{E}$. We construct $E^\tau = \tau E + (1-\tau)E'$

for $\tau \in [0,1]$, i.e., $E^{\tau} = (\gamma^{\tau}, u^{\tau}, \bar{x}^{\tau}, \bar{m}^{\tau}) = (\tau\gamma + (1-\tau)\gamma', \tau u + (1-\tau)u', \tau\bar{x} + (1-\tau)\bar{x}', \tau\bar{m} + (1-\tau)\bar{m}')$. By the "weak" topology given on $\mathscr{E}$, it is easy to see that $\gamma^{h\tau} \in \Gamma$, $u^{h\tau} \in \mathscr{U}$, $\bar{x}^{h\tau} \in P$ and $\bar{m}^{h\tau} \in R_{+}$ for every h. Hence $E^{\tau} \in \mathscr{E}$ (compare with the proof of Theorem 3). From definition of the map ψ_E and Propositon 11, ψ_E^{*} is proper. In particular $\psi_E^{-1}(0)$ is compact and boundaryless in $P^n \times F \times \Pi$. By Proposition 13, there exists $E \in \mathscr{R} \subset \mathscr{E}$ such that the Brouwer degree of the map ψ_E, denoted $\deg \psi_E$, is one. Furthermore, the Brouwer degree is homotopy invariant, hence $\deg \psi_E$ is one for every $E \in \mathscr{E}$. This implies $\psi_E^{-1}(0) \neq \phi$ and hence $\Phi(E) = \psi_E^{-1}(0) \neq \phi$ for every $E \in \mathscr{E}$. Q.E.D.

COROLLARY 6. <u>For every classical money economy with spot and futures transactions, there exists temporary monetary equilibrium, i.e.,</u> $W(E) \neq \phi$ <u>for all</u> $E \in \mathscr{E}_0$.

Chapter VI

CONCLUSION: SUGGESTIONS FOR FUTURE RESEARCH

In this research, we studied the non-voidness and the structure of the set of short-run or temporary monetary equilibria. The latter includes mainly the local uniqueness and stability of equilibria. As discussed, a temporary equilibrium theory can be viewed as a general Walrasian equilibrium analysis of a sequence of markets over time, where at each date each agent makes decisions according to his expectations of the future environment. These expectations are formed in the light of the agent's knowledge of current and past information. Our study has emphasized introducing a financial asset called "money" into the model. Then a temporary monetary equilibrium is defined as a temporary equilibrium situation with positive price of money, although money has no intrinsic value for consumption. In general, the agent's expectations are often not only the expectations of future prices and endowments, but also the expectations of market conditions, demand, and supply of others, for example. This introduces the possibility of externalities into the formulation. The analysis carries over without any problem to such a generalization. The other examples are the appearance of transaction costs and quantity constraints on transactions in the model. The latter especially brings the Keynesian flavor into a microeconomic context, and attempts have been made so as to prove the existence of temporary Keynesian equilibrium using standard fixed point arguments (see [4] and [24], among others). A further investigation along this line could be to find restrictions on a rationing mechanism in a temporary Keynesian model so that some determinate equilibrium properties are preserved in a differentiable framework (see also [43]). On the other hand, under the case of certainty, the existence problem of a sequential Arrow-Debreu economy with transaction costs has been answered in [31], [41], and [42], among others. An alternative approach to studying the non-emptyness and the structure of the set of equilibria with transaction costs under uncertainty is to view the economic system as a sequence of temporary equilibria.

Although time has been incorporated explicitly into the temporary equilibrium analysis, the model is essentially a static one which ensures the equilibrium properties only in a temporary sense. That is, disequilibrium phenomena in the future are allowed and left unanswered. Future work for pursuing the properties of a sequence of temporary equilibria over periods are suggested; in particular, establishing conditions such that a locally unique and stable temporary equilibrium at present gives rise to an economic environment for which a locally unique and stable equilibrium exists in the future. The equilibria obtained are not necessarily stationary. Furthermore, it is well known that a sequence of temporary equilibria in general is not Pareto optimal, and hence the core may not be equivalent to the set of equilibrium allocations even in a large economy. It would be interesting to search for assumptions such that the sequence of temporary equilibria is optimal in a Pareto sense and the core converges to the set of equilibrium allocations as the number of agents tends to infinity. In a differentiable framework, we also expect, under the same conditions (if any), that for every regular economy there exists a diffeomorphism assigning equilibrium allocations to Pareto optima, and that the core converges like the inverse of the number of agents. (See [54], [12], [51], [52], [12], and [30] for discussions of analogous results in the Arrow-Debreu general equilibrium model.)

REFERENCES

1. Abraham, R. and J. Robbin, Transversal Mappings and Flows, W.A. Benjamin, Inc., New York, 1967.

2. Arrow, K.J. and F.H. Hahn, General Competitive Analysis, Holden-Day, San Francisco, 1971.

3. Balasko, Y., "Some Results on Uniqueness and Stability of Equilibrium in General Equilibrium Theory", Journal of Mathematical Economics 2, 1975, pp. 95-118.

4. Benassy, J.-P., "Neo-Keynesian Disequilibrium Theory in a Monetary Economy", Review of Economic Studies 42, 1975, pp. 503-523.

5. Billingsley, P., Convergence of Probability Measures, Wiley, New York, 1968.

6. Christiansen, D.S. and M. Majumdar, "On Shifting Temporary Equilibrium", Department of Economics, Cornell University, 1974.

7. Debreu, G., Theory of Value, Wiley, New York, 1959.

8. Debreu, G., "Neighboring Economic Agents", in La Decision, Editions du Centre National de la Recherche Scientifique, pp. 85-90, Paris, 1969.

9. Debreu, G., "Economies with a Finite Set of Equilibria", Econometrica 38, 1970, pp. 387-392.

10. Debreu, G., "Smooth Preferences", Econometrica 40, 1972, pp. 603-615.

11. Debreu, G., "The Rate of Convergence of the Core of an Economy", Journal of Mathematical Economics 2, 1975, pp. 1-7.

12. Debreu, G. and H. Scarf, "A Limit Theorem on the Core of an Economy", International Economic Review 4, 1963, pp. 235-246.

13. Dierker, E. and H. Dierker, "On the Local Uniqueness of Equilibria", Econometrica 40, 1972, pp. 867-881.

14. Dierker, E., Topological Methods in Walrasian Economics Springer-Verlag, 1974.

15. Dieudonne, J., Foundation of Modern Analysis, Academic Press, New York, 1960.

16. Dusansky, R. and P.J. Kalman, "The Real Balance Effect and the Traditional Theory of Consumer Behavior: A Reconciliation", Journal of Economic Theory 5, 1972, pp. 336-347.

17. Dusansky, R. and P.J. Kalman, "The Foundations of Money Illusion in a Neoclassical Micro-Monetary Model", American Economic Review LXIV, March 1974, pp. 115-122.

18. Fuchs, G., "Private Ownership Economies with a Finite Number of Equilibria", Journal of Mathematical Economics 1, 1974, pp. 141-158.

19. Fuchs, G. and G. Laroque, "Dynamics of Temporary Equilibria and Expectations", Econometrica 44, 1976.

20. Grandmont, J.-M., "On the Short-Run Equilibrium in a Monetary Economy", in J. Drezé (ed.), Allocation Under Uncertainty: Equilibrium and Optimality, Macmillan, New York, 1974, pp. 213-228.

21. Grandmont, J.-M. and W. Hildenbrand, "Stochastic Processes of Temporary Equilibria", Journal of Mathematical Economics 1, 1974, pp. 247-277.

22. Grandmont, J.-M. and G. Laroque, "Money in the Pure Consumption Loan Model", Journal of Economic Theory 6, 1973, pp. 382-395.

23. Grandmont, J.-M. and G. Laroque, "The Liquidity Trap", Econometrica 44, 1976, pp. 129-135.

24. Grandmont, J.-M. and G. Laroque, "On Temporary Keynesian Equilibria", Review of Economic Studies 43, 1976, pp. 53-67.

25. Grandmont, J.-M. and Y. Younès, "On the Role of Money and the Existence of a Monetary Equilibrium", Review of Economic Studies 39, 1972, pp. 355-372.

26. Grandmont, J.-M. and Y. Younès, "On the Efficiency of a Monetary Equilibrium", Review of Economic Studies 40, 1973, pp. 149-165.

27. Green, J.R., "Temporary General Equilibrium in a Sequential Trading Model with Spot and Future Transactions", Econometrica 41, 1973, pp. 1103-1124.

28. Green, J.R., "Preexisting Contracts and Temporary General Equilibrium", in M. Balch, D. Mcfadden and S.W. Yu (eds.), Essays on Economic Behavior under Uncertainty, North-Holland, 1974, pp. 263-286.

29. Grodal, B., "A Note on the Space of Preference Relations", Journal of Mathematical Economics 1, 1974, pp. 279-294.

30. Grodal, B., "The Rate of Convergence of the Core for a Pure Competitive Sequence of Economies", Journal of Mathematical Economics 2, 1975, pp. 171-186.

31. Hahn, R.H., "Equilibrium with Transaction Costs", Econometrica 39, 1971, pp. 417-439.

32. Hicks, J., Value and Capital, Clarendon Press, 1946.

33. Hildenbrand, W., "On Economies with Many Agents", Journal of Economic Theory 2, 1970, pp. 161-188.

34. Hirsch, M.W., Differential Topology, Springer-Verlag, 1976.

35. Hool, R.B., "Temporary Walrasian Equilibrium in a Monetary Economy", in Adaptive Economic Models, R.H. Day and T. Groves (eds.), Academic Press, New York, 1975, pp. 499-512.

36. Kalman, P.J., "Theory of Consumer Behavior when Prices Enter the Utility Function", Econometrica 36, 1968, pp. 497-510.

37. Kannai, Y., "Continuity Properties of the Core of a Market", Econometrica 38, 1970, pp. 791-815.

38. Kannai, Y., "Approximation of Convex Preferences", Journal of Mathematical Economics 1, 1974, pp. 101-106.

39. Katzner, D.W., "A Note on the Differentiability of Consumer Demand Functions", Econometrica 36, 1968, pp. 415-418.

40. Kelley, J., General Topology, Van Nostrand, Princeton, 1960.

41. Kurz, M., "Equilibrium with Transaction Cost and Money in a Single-Market Exchange Economy", Journal of Economic Theory 7, 1974, pp. 333-368.

42. Kurz, M., "Arrow-Debreu Equilibrium of an Exchange Economy with Transaction Cost", International Economic Review 15, 1974, pp. 699-717.

43. Laroque, G. and H. Polemarchakis, "On the Structure of the Set of Fixed Price Equilibria", Harvard University, 1976.

44. Mas-Collel, A., "Continuous and Smooth Consumers: Approximation Theorems", Journal of Economic Theory 8, 1974, pp. 305-336.

45. Milnor, J., Topology from a Differentiable Viewpoint, University of Virginia Press, 1965.

46. Parthasarathy, K.R., Probability Measures on Metric Space, Academic Press, 1967.

47. Patinkin, D., Money, Interest and Price, Harper and Row, 1965.

48. Peixoto, M.M., "On an Approximation Theorem of Kupka and Smale", Journal of Differential Equations 3, 1966, pp. 214-227.

49. Samuelson, P.A., The Foundations of Economic Analysis, Harvard University Press, Cambridge, Mass., 1947.

50. Scitovsky, T., "Some Consequences of Habit of Judging Quality by Price", Review of Economic Studies 12, 1945, pp. 100-105.

51. Shapley, L.S. and M. Shubik, "Pure Competition, Coalition Power, and Fair Division", International Economic Review 10, 1969, pp. 337-362.

52. Shapley, L.S., "An Example of a Slow-Converging Core", International Economic Review 16, 1975.

53. Smale, S., "Global Analysis and Economics IIA: Extensions of a Theorem of Debreu", Journal of Mathematical Economics 1, 1974, pp. 1-14.

54. Smale, S., "Global Analysis and Economics III: Pareto Optima and Price Equilibria", Journal of Mathematical Economics 1, 1974, pp. 107-117.

55. Smale, S., "Global Analysis and Economics IV: Finiteness and Stability of Equilibria with General Consumption Sets and Production", Journal of Mathematical Economics 1, 1974, pp. 119-127.

56. Sondermann, D., "Temporary Competitive Equilibrium Under Uncertainty", in J. Dreze (ed.), Allocation Under Uncertainty: Equilibrium and Optimality, Macmillan, New York, 1974, pp. 229-253.

57. Stigum, B.P., "Competitive Equilibria under Uncertainty", Quarterly Journal of Economics 83, 1969, pp. 533-561.

58. Stigum, B.P., "Resource Allocation under Uncertainty", International Economic Review 13, 1972, pp. 431-459.

59. Veblen, T., The Theory of the Leisure Class, Macmillan, New York, 1899.

60. Wallace, A.H., Algebraic Topology: Homology and Cohomology, Benjamin, New York, 1970.

61. Younès, Y., "Money and Interest in a Walrasian Short-Run Equilibrium", MSSB Working Paper, University of California, Berkeley, 1973.

For Product Safety Concerns and Information please contact our EU representative GPSR@taylorandfrancis.com Taylor & Francis Verlag GmbH, Kaufingerstraße 24, 80331 München, Germany